New Urban Geographies of the Creative and Knowledge Economies

The temporal and spatial intersection of information and telecommunication technologies, creative and knowledge economies, and related new manufacturing systems, has been leading to significant effects on urban socioeconomic and spatial configurations and public policies. Specifically, the post-crisis emergence of innovative workplaces to accommodate these changes, is creating socioeconomic and spatial features that are only recently beginning to be explored in the scholarly literature.

According to this scenario, this edited book offers a variety of avenues for exploring the relationships between contemporary production activities and new workplaces in several urban contexts. In particular, it focuses on the consequences of these relationships in terms of regeneration of the urban fabric, as well as on their implication in terms of urban policies.

This book represents early observation of the fast-growing phenomenon of new productive activities and workplaces against the background of the gig economy and sharing economy paradigms. Central to this discussion is the investigation of the connection between digital technologies, new works and workplaces, and urban change processes and projects, by providing an additional contribution to new urban agendas for contemporary cities.

The chapters in this book were originally published as a special issue of the *Journal of Urban Technology*.

Simonetta Armondi is Assistant Professor of Political and Economic Geography in the Department of Architecture and Urban Studies at the Politecnico di Milano, Italy.

Stefano Di Vita is Adjunct Professor of Urban Planning and Design in the Department of Architecture and Urban Studies at the Politecnico di Milano, Italy.

New Urban Geographies of the Creative and Knowledge Economies

Foregrounding Innovative Productions, Workplaces and Public Policies in Contemporary Cities

Edited by
Simonetta Armondi and Stefano Di Vita

LONDON AND NEW YORK

First published 2018
by Routledge
2 Park Square, Milton Park, Abingdon, Oxon, OX14 4RN, UK

and by Routledge
711 Third Avenue, New York, NY 10017, USA

Routledge is an imprint of the Taylor & Francis Group, an informa business

© 2018 The Society of Urban Technology

All rights reserved. No part of this book may be reprinted or reproduced or utilised in any form or by any electronic, mechanical, or other means, now known or hereafter invented, including photocopying and recording, or in any information storage or retrieval system, without permission in writing from the publishers.

Trademark notice: Product or corporate names may be trademarks or registered trademarks, and are used only for identification and explanation without intent to infringe.

British Library Cataloguing in Publication Data
A catalogue record for this book is available from the British Library

ISBN 13: 978-0-8153-5882-4

Typeset in Minion Pro
by RefineCatch Limited, Bungay, Suffolk

Publisher's Note
The publisher accepts responsibility for any inconsistencies that may have arisen during the conversion of this book from journal articles to book chapters, namely the possible inclusion of journal terminology.

Disclaimer
Every effort has been made to contact copyright holders for their permission to reprint material in this book. The publishers would be grateful to hear from any copyright holder who is not here acknowledged and will undertake to rectify any errors or omissions in future editions of this book.

Contents

Citation Information vii
Notes on Contributors ix
Acknowledgement xi

1. Contemporary Production, Innovative Workplaces, and Urban Space: Projects and Policies 1
   Simonetta Armondi and Stefano Di Vita

2. Emerging Workplaces in Post-Functionalist Cities 5
   Mina Di Marino and Kimmo Lapintie

3. Contemporary Production and Urban Change: The Case of Milan 27
   Simonetta Armondi and Antonella Bruzzese

4. Co-working Spaces in Milan: Location Patterns and Urban Effects 47
   Ilaria Mariotti, Carolina Pacchi, and Stefano Di Vita

5. Hubs of Internet Entrepreneurs: The Emergence of Co-working Offices in Shanghai, China 67
   Bo Wang and Becky P. Y. Loo

6. Why Knowledge Megaprojects Will Fail to Transform Gulf Countries in Post-Carbon Economies: The Case of Qatar 85
   Agatino Rizzo

7. Catch Me if You Can: Workplace Mobility and Big Data 99
   Filipa Pajević and Richard G. Shearmur

Index 117

Citation Information

The chapters in this book were originally published in the *Journal of Urban Technology*, volume 24, issue 3 (July 2017). When citing this material, please use the original page numbering for each article, as follows:

Chapter 1
Contemporary Production, Innovative Workplaces, and Urban Space: Projects and Policies
Simonetta Armondi and Stefano Di Vita
Journal of Urban Technology, volume 24, issue 3 (July 2017), pp. 1–4

Chapter 2
Emerging Workplaces in Post-Functionalist Cities
Mina Di Marino and Kimmo Lapintie
Journal of Urban Technology, volume 24, issue 3 (July 2017), pp. 5–26

Chapter 3
Contemporary Production and Urban Change: The Case of Milan
Simonetta Armondi and Antonella Bruzzese
Journal of Urban Technology, volume 24, issue 3 (July 2017), pp. 27–46

Chapter 4
Co-working Spaces in Milan: Location Patterns and Urban Effects
Ilaria Mariotti, Carolina Pacchi, and Stefano Di Vita
Journal of Urban Technology, volume 24, issue 3 (July 2017), pp. 47–66

Chapter 5
Hubs of Internet Entrepreneurs: The Emergence of Co-working Offices in Shanghai, China
Bo Wang and Becky P. Y. Loo
Journal of Urban Technology, volume 24, issue 3 (July 2017), pp. 67–84

Chapter 6
Why Knowledge Megaprojects Will Fail to Transform Gulf Countries in Post-Carbon Economies: The Case of Qatar
Agatino Rizzo
Journal of Urban Technology, volume 24, issue 3 (July 2017), pp. 85–98

CITATION INFORMATION

Chapter 7
Catch Me if You Can: Workplace Mobility and Big Data
Filipa Pajević and Richard G. Shearmur
Journal of Urban Technology, volume 24, issue 3 (July 2017), pp. 99–116

For any permission-related enquiries please visit:
http://www.tandfonline.com/page/help/permissions

Notes on Contributors

Simonetta Armondi is Assistant Professor of Political and Economic Geography in the Department of Architecture and Urban Studies at the Politecnico di Milano, Italy.

Antonella Bruzzese is Associate Professor of Urban Planning in the Department of Architecture and Urban Studies, Politecnico di Milano, Italy.

Mina Di Marino is Associate Professor of Urban and Regional Planning in the Department of Urban and Regional Planning, Norwegian University of Life Sciences, Ås, Norway.

Stefano Di Vita is Adjunct Professor of Urban Planning and Design in the Department of Architecture and Urban Studies at the Politecnico di Milano, Italy.

Kimmo Lapintie is Professor of Urban and Regional Planning and Head of Research at the Department of Architecture, Aalto University, Finland.

Becky P. Y. Loo is Professor at the Department of Geography, The University of Hong Kong, Hong Kong. Her current research interests are transportation, e-technologies and society.

Ilaria Mariotti is Associate Professor of Urban Regional Economics in the Department of Architecture and Urban Studies at the Politecnico di Milano, Italy.

Carolina Pacchi is Associate Professor of Urban Planning and Design in the Department of Architecture and Urban Studies at the Politecnico di Milano, Italy.

Filipa Pajević is a PhD student at the School of Urban Planning, McGill University, Canada. Her research interests cover the spatial dynamics of mobile and multi-locational workers, knowledge and "gig" work, and new working environments.

Agatino Rizzo is Associate Professor of Urban Planning and Design in the Architecture Research Group at Luleå University of Technology, Sweden. His main research interest is resource-based urbanization in connection with cross-cutting themes such as resilience, climate, development, politics, and energy.

Richard G. Shearmur is Professor of Urban and Regional Economics at the School of Urban Planning, McGill University, Canada. He has published extensively on the location of jobs in metropolitan areas and on the connection between innovation processes and space.

Bo Wang is a Research Fellow at the Department of Geography, The University of Hong Kong, Hong Kong.

Acknowledgement

A special thank you to Richard Hanley, editor of the *Journal of Urban Technology*, who made this publication possible.

Contemporary Production, Innovative Workplaces, and Urban Space: Projects and Policies

Simonetta Armondi and Stefano Di Vita

The temporal and spatial intersection of information and telecommunication technologies, creative- and knowledge-based economies, and new manufacturing systems has had a significant effect on urban spatial configurations. Specifically, the emergence of innovative workplaces to accommodate these changes, such as co-working spaces, "Fab-Labs," and the like is creating spatial and socioeconomic features that are only recently beginning to be explored in the scholarly literature.

The papers in this issue offer a variety of avenues for exploring the relationships between production activities and new workplaces. They also explore the spatial consequences of these relationships for the urban fabric. The papers address a variety of research questions regarding these new places of production:

- What are the characteristics of the urban locations of these workplaces? Do these locations enhance knowledge dissemination? Foster innovation at the urban level? Sustain productivity growth?
- What are their socioeconomic effects on cities or urban neighborhoods?
- Are these workplaces transforming urban spaces? In what ways?
- How are urban policy makers responding to these innovative spaces? What policies, planning tools, or strategic approaches are being applied to these venues?
- Can urban policies, plans, or projects slow down or accelerate the expansion of these dynamic workplaces?

The issue's first article "Emerging Workplaces in Post-Functionalist Cities" by Mina Di Marino and Kimmo Lapintie focuses on the growth of temporary work locations that house flexible contemporary work activities made possible by information and communication technologies. These specialized co-working spaces include different kinds of public and semi-public spaces (such as libraries or coffee shops). The authors explore this phenomenon in three locations in the city center of Helsinki, and they highlight the need for urban policies and practices that will deal with the growing blurring of boundaries between traditional urban functions.

In their article "Contemporary Production and Urban Change: The Case of Milan," Simonetta Armondi and Antonella Bruzzese study not a city center, but the periphery of the city of Milan. They examine how municipal public policies belonging to the smart city agenda, on the one hand, and cultural and creative industries promoted by private operators on the other, can lead to the development of new kinds of production and innovative workplaces. Their analysis teases out the differences and potential combined effects of public actions and private initiatives, focusing in particular on their outcomes in terms of social inclusion and place-making in the peripheral areas of Milan.

The authors Ilaria Mariotti, Carolina Pacchi, and Stefano Di Vita also use Milan as the locus of their study. In their article, "Co-Working Spaces in Milan: Location Patterns and Urban Effects," the authors investigate one manifestation of these innovative workplaces—co-working spaces—to see if they can discern a relationship between these spaces and urban regeneration. They focus particularly on their location patterns and their effects on the urban context, both in terms of urban spaces and practices.

In their article, Bo Wang and Becky P.Y. Loo look at this same phenomenon as it is manifested in a radically different political, economic, and social context than Milan. In "Hubs of Internet Entrepreneurs: The Emergence of Co-Working Offices in Shanghai, China" Wang and Loo analyze the growth of co-working spaces in Shanghai. Their contribution examines the geographical factors, as well as the reasons and processes for the development of these innovative workplaces, whose growth is supported by government policies at both the national and local levels as well as by strong market demand for what the Chinese call "Internet plus" entrepreneurs.

Unlike most of the studies in this issue, Agatino Rizzo's urban study does not focus on a single building, block, or neighborhood. In "Why Knowledge Megaprojects Will Fail to Transform Gulf Countries in Post-Carbon Economies: The Case of Qatar" he deals with the ongoing increase in cognitive cultural capitalism from a radically different perspective, shifting from the molecular intervention of recycling singular buildings and spaces for new uses to mega-projects. The article analyzes the case of the Education City developed by the government of Qatar in Doha. This contribution highlights the contradictions of huge interventions, the method that Gulf countries use to support their diversification from fossil fuels to a knowledge economy. The problem, as Rizzo outlines it, is that this method replicates the same shortcomings of their other large, unsuccessful urban development initiatives.

In "Catch Me if You Can: Workplace Mobility and Big Data," Filipa Pajević and Richard G. Shearmur, instead of focusing on specific innovative workplaces or case studies, add a final reflection about the general issues concerning the multiple locations of growing numbers of knowledge workers. By exploiting the potentials of information and communication technologies, which enable the daytime workplace mobility explored in other articles in this issue, this contribution explains how Big Data, generated by digital technologies, can shed light on the urban trajectories of mobile workers, which are otherwise difficult to capture through traditional analyses.

The papers in this issue represent early explorations of the fast-growing phenomenon of new urban workspaces. Central to these discussions is the exploration of the connection between these innovative technologies, new workspaces, governmental policies and urban space—and, perhaps, urban transformation. In short, this focus issue is an additional contribution to a new, critical, urban agenda.

During the writing process, we benefited from the support of Richard Hanley, editor of the journal, whose advice has been of incommensurable value. We are also very grateful both to the anonymous referees who evaluated the first versions of the manuscripts, and to Jessica Ferm and Bruno Moriset, who thoroughly reviewed two books (Mason et al., 2015; Gandini, 2016) strongly related to the topics of this focus issue and, accordingly, included in it.

ORCID

Simonetta Armondi http://orcid.org/0000-0001-5293-7581

Bibliography

A. Gandini, *The Reputation Economy: Understanding Knowledge Work in Digital Society* (London: Palgrave McMillan, 2016).

C. Mason, D. Reuschke, S. Syrett, and M. van Ham, eds, *Entrepreneurship in Cities: Neighbourhoods, Households, and Homes* (Cheltenham: Elgar, 2015).

Emerging Workplaces in Post-Functionalist Cities

Mina Di Marino and Kimmo Lapintie

ABSTRACT
This paper explores new types of workplaces that are emerging due to the growing flexibility in work arrangements and the use of information and communication technologies. In addition to home and office, third places, such as libraries and coffee shops, are increasingly used as temporary workplaces. Moreover, there is a proliferation of co-working spaces that are designed as temporary working locations. Thus, the boundaries between traditional urban functions have become blurred; different functions co-exist in the same spaces, and new functionalities emerge as people take spaces into new uses. We may call our cities "post-functionalist," ones that are no longer based only on predetermined and designed functions. However, there has been little research on the spatial characteristics of these new workplaces as well as on the social features within these places. These phenomena have been empirically studied through observational studies, interviews, and spatial analyses of three such sites: Café Köket, Meetingpoint, and Helsinki Think Company in the city center of Helsinki. The results reveal new forms of appropriation of public and semi-public spaces for working purposes that have not yet been analyzed in the context of existing urban policies and practices. The findings provide input for future visions and the planning of new workplaces.

Introduction

Recently, scholars have focused on the role of coffee shops, libraries, and co-working spaces as emerging spaces for working (Sanusi and Palen, 2008; Bilandzic and Foth, 2013; Gandini, 2015). The changed use of these spaces has occurred for several reasons: Working practices are changing and becoming more flexible (Pyöriä, 2003), there is growing access to private and public Wi-Fi (Grubesic and Murray, 2004), and public and semi-public spaces provide new services and make facilities that make working outside the office easier and more convenient.

Libraries and coffee shops have acted as third places for their capacity to facilitate interactions as well as create a feeling of being at home while away from home (Oldenburg, 1999, 2001). However, third places have recently been considered more than merely informal public gathering places or places of consumption. Indeed, libraries and coffee shops are not usually designed for working activities; nevertheless, they are increasingly emerging as spaces for work. Libraries, for instance, have adapted to the digital age by offering new spaces, technologies, and services and, more recently, by providing co-working spaces (Bilandzic and Foth, 2013; Houghton et al., 2013). In addition, coffee shops are used for a variety of purposes, such as informal offices. There has been an apparent lack of access to office equipment in coffee shops, but information technologies are also now provided in these spaces (Brown and O'Hara, 2003) with some coffee shops providing facilities for working, such as meeting rooms, printers, projectors, and Wi-Fi.

Unlike coffee shops and libraries, co-working spaces are specifically designed as temporary working locations by providing desks and meeting rooms, as well as by offering opportunities to network and develop start-ups (Moriset, 2015). Unlike third places, co-working spaces are conceived as "territories that are accessed purposely to construct and maintain network relations and perpetrate a market position" (Gandini, 2015: 200). Co-working environments are mostly seen as spaces for urban-based freelancers who work halfway between well-delimited workplace and home, the so-called "third way" (Gandini, 2015). However, most of the buildings that currently host co-working spaces were originally designed for other functions, such as factories and commercial spaces. Presently, industrial loft spaces answer the needs and requirements of co-working spaces and activities. Furthermore, there is a proliferation of paid co-working spaces, while only a few co-working spaces are provided free by cities or public universities.

In architecture and planning, although the functionalistic division of urban spaces into the basic functions of housing, work, leisure, and mobility has been criticized since the 1980s, it still dominates land-use planning. In this study, the concept of the post-functionalist city is used to denote a city where the boundaries between urban functions have become blurred, where different functions co-exist in the same space, and where new and unprecedented functions emerge through citizens' appropriation of places. It can be seen in the context of the current debate on functional city versus connected city (Davoudi and Madanipour, 2012; Tummers and Zibell, 2012; Neal, 2013). The idea of a functional city, with its separation of functions, has been replaced in the New Charter of Athens (2003) with the concept of a connected city with its goal of integrating and implying new mixtures of land-use (Tummers and Zibell, 2012). However, thus far, scholars have stated that the concept of the connected city has not effectively responded to the current challenges, such as urban fragmentation, public participation, globalization and the use of ICT. The New Charter gives an unrealistic vision when it describes different groups of residents in the connected city, both temporary and permanent, who would be content with using urban services without wanting to participate in local decision-making (Davoudi and Madanipour, 2012). Temporary residents, for instance, can spend long periods in second homes; thus implying a call to identify the local decision-making processes in which they might participate (Weichart, 2015). In addition, the polycentric urban networks, which are part of the connected city, are meant to network several flows, but the New Charter does not mention the flow of commuting residents (Tummers and Zibell, 2012). However, the micro-urban network of commuting workers, as well as the activities that are concentrated in multiple places have been recently explored within the connected city (Nael, 2013). When the New Charter tries to portray the "social connectivity," it mostly refers to the improvement of physical structures for mobility and movement (Tummers and Zibell, 2012), while the role of digital infrastructures is not clear (Fernandez-Maldonado, 2012).

Spatial planners have produced the New Charter mainly in order to avoid a blueprint approach (Davoudi and Madanipour, 2012). However, most of the current planning approaches and instruments are still based on the concept of the functional city (Tummers and Zibell, 2012). In fact, we still see the predominance of the functionalist tradition in mainstream thinking about design and planning. To this end, there has been an extensive debate about multi-functionality in modern cities. While several suburban areas are less multifunctional and more homogenous, spatial patterns are much more complicated when related to older neighborhoods and city centers (Batty et al., 2004). In the current circumstances, an increasing number of people are able to arrange their work around their access to different uses and activities in time and space (Batty et al., 2004). However, we still need to collect data to clearly picture the transformation cities are undergoing.

Alternative resilient approaches where the designer's imagination of what will happen, or how users will use the urban spaces, are needed. Even the concept of mixed-use implies designating a number of imagined functions to the built environment, whereas designing the post-functionalist city would call for flexibility and the opening of possibilities that are not yet determined. The post-functionalist city still serves several functions for society, but its spaces are increasingly often characterized as multifunctional, mixed, and changing. A post-functionalist city refers to a city where the functional definition of spaces, as well as the functionalist design of these spaces, is becoming obsolete. New forms of appropriation are occurring, such as working and living in multiple places. However, this phenomenon has not been analyzed in the context of existing urban policies and practices.

The emerging workplaces embrace public spaces, such as libraries, as well as semi-public spaces, such as coffee shops, that are not planned to host work functions, but are increasingly used as spaces to work. The co-working spaces are also considered as emerging workplaces. Co-working spaces are mostly located within industrial and commercial buildings that have been turned into non-traditional offices. This study focuses on co-working spaces provided as public services by cities and public universities. We state that coffee shops, libraries, and co-working spaces can be seen as temporary and hybrid new workspaces for individuals and groups of workers, as well as creative places for artists, freelancers, and start-up businesses. However, there is not much research on the spatial characteristics of these new workplaces within cities, nor on the social and relational features within these places. Thus, this paper addresses the following research questions: (1) What are the spatial characteristics of the emerging workplaces in urban settings, and accordingly, what is the context of existing urban policies and practices? (2) Why do people choose these places to work? To address these research questions, the study presents a comprehensive literature review that first focuses on the interpretations of public, semi-public, and private spheres and space and, second, on the ways information and communication technologies (ICT) can transform the use of urban spaces. Third, the literature review focuses on the use of coffee shops, libraries, and co-working spaces as temporary and hybrid workplaces. As case studies, three places are investigated that are located in the Helsinki city center: Café Köket; Meeting Point (an urban office provided by the Helsinki City Library); and Helsinki Think Company (co-working space provided by the City of Helsinki and the University of Helsinki). The reason for selecting the three cases is the growing interest in the development of alternative workplaces such as these among local authorities as well as stakeholders, including entrepreneurs, managers, and directors of these facilities. The findings from this study will contribute to the current theoretical debate about the change in the traditional functionalist understanding of the use of urban spaces. This study will also be relevant to the future visioning, planning, and design of urban spaces.

Background

Public, Semi-Public, and Private Spaces

Scholars from several disciplines have focused on the interpretation of public, semi-public, and private spaces. In order to define these spaces, academics have considered multiple aspects, including the type of access, spatial and time configurations, groups of actors, individual behavior, type of control (by public or private sectors) and, more recently, the multiple uses of spaces (e.g., see the overview provided by Mehta, 2014). Often the conceptual boundaries between public and private dimensions are not delineated.

In this context, architects and planners have delivered several socio-spatial interpretations. For example, the private and public spheres in the cities used to depend on the boundaries that separate them. "The space of the city is shaped by many forms and levels of boundaries ... " (Madanipour, 2003: 60). The barriers that have been represented through multi-level configurations and meanings (such as physical boundaries, norms, and behavior) are meant to shape spatial arrangements and social relationships between public and private realms (Madanipour, 2003). Public spaces are not only conceived as monumental spaces or as venues for public discourses and festivals, but they are also designed to be urban settings of everyday life, as well as spaces for communication and social encounters (Banerjee, 2001; Carmona, 2015). However, several public spaces of the city are abandoned or they have become places to pass through (Carmona 2003, Madanipour 2003, Gehl 2011).

Furthermore, the level of sociability seems to decrease within the public and semi-public spaces in favor of being in silence (Madanipour, 2003). There is also a tendency to protect the intimate personal space of the body into its physical surrounding (Madanipour, 2003). On the other hand, passive contact in public and semi-public spaces, such as hearing others and being among unknown people, can be seen as a source of inspiration, as well as "a possibility of maintaining already established contacts" (Gehl, 2011: 15).

Semi-public spaces are those spaces accessible to the public but privately managed and controlled. The overview given by Hampton (2008) shows that semi-public spaces have changed meanings and roles. Referring to Lofland (1973), he stated that semi-public spaces cannot be completely seen as a "world of strangers" or domesticated spaces. Habermas (1989) argued that semi-public spaces, such as coffee shops, used to play a key role in the development of a public sphere for a social and political debate. Afterwards, semi-public spaces were still considered important to social life, but they were mostly identified as venues creating a sense of place and community (Oldenburg, 1999). The overview by Hampton (2008) concludes with a statement, which is currently shared by several academics: that the modern urban environment contributes to the current isolation and social segregation in both public and semi-public spaces.

The growing interferences and interdependencies between private and public spheres have often resulted in the unclear distinction between spaces for private life, work, and leisure. More recently, modern information and communication technologies have contributed to blurring these boundaries (Vartiainen and Hyrkkänen, 2010; Koroma et al., 2014). Architects and planners need to gain a broader perspective and knowledge by adding the role of technologies to socio-spatial interpretations.

Urban Spaces and Information and Communication Technologies

The latest changes in Information and Communication Technologies have revolutionized the functional differentiation of urban spaces. Since the late 1990s, people have increasingly arranged time and place through mobile technologies. Previous studies on mobile communications have tried to direct attention to those places that people use to work (Townsend, 2000; Brown and O'Hara, 2003; Willis, 2008). The Nordic countries have been involved from early on in the deployment and adoption of mobile technologies. Referring to Kopomaa, Townsend (2000) remarked that the mobile phone represents a "postmodern form of communication" that affects the use of public and private spaces within a certain time. In particular, Townsend (2000) argued that the networks with friends and colleagues using mobile phones have permitted a reshaping of time and spatial configurations. This happens particularly with workers who require the network "to be on the go and in touch with a home base" (2000: 10). In these times, modern telecommunication and information technologies allow communities to be virtual. This means, for instance, being in contact with others far away. However, the Internet also allows groups to have more local contacts, both virtual and physical (Schwanen and Kwan, 2008).

Academics have been studying the larger impacts of mobile technologies on urban spaces and cities (e.g., Foth and Sunders, 2008; Al-Kodmany, 2012). More recently, smartphones, tablets, and Wi-Fi, in addition to laptops, have inserted a decisive impulse to the mobile lifestyle (Forlano, 2015). Internet use is no longer limited to home and the workplace; it is increasingly part of our everyday life on the streets and in other public and semi-public spaces (Hampton et al., 2010). Municipal governments support the deployment of Wi-Fi for city employees and broadband access to local populations, such as Wi-Fi hotspots and Park Wi-Fi (Ganapati and Shoepp, 2008; Bar and Park, 2006). The prevailing idea is to improve the synergies between traditional city services and network access (Hartmann, 2009). Interestingly, residents, visitors, and workers benefit from modern telecommunications and ICT infrastructures that public and private spaces have increasingly offered (Grubesic and Murray, 2004).

Apparently, this calls for a new understanding of urban spaces. In architecture and urban design, space has traditionally been defined in material and aesthetic terms by some implicit social characteristics that are supported by design (e.g., representational, commercial, or recreational). In planning and urban studies, on the other hand, space has been given a more social and political meaning through concepts such as segregation, gentrification, and exclusion. However, these characterizations have often lacked a sufficient connectedness to the physical characteristics of places. Although these interpretations of space are by themselves problematic (Lapintie, 2007), the advent of mobile technologies has brought in more complications. Urban spaces are increasingly characterized by access to virtual networks through public and private Wi-Fi spots, and the spaces around these spots do not respect material boundaries (Willis, 2008; Castells, 2011). However, they are locational, thus implying that the common view of being connected everywhere and anytime is misleading (Grubesic and Murray, 2004). Instead, we can say that central city areas are dominant even with respect to this new form of infrastructure, while more remote areas have to be satisfied with slower 3G-networks, or lack connections altogether.

The social and functional characteristics of urban spaces are naturally affected by access to virtual networks. It has become possible to co-work in several places that have not been designed for working purposes. Consequently, these places have become more attractive, even for those who prefer working alone in a crowd. There is also a need to see virtual connections as an elemental part of urban spaces in the sense that they provide virtual access to places and people outside the actual place (Castells, 2011). The users of urban space are surrounded by three types of accessibility: the physical space consisting of the current place in use (and possessing certain characteristics which determine the activities that can reasonably be performed in that place, as well as the people who can be met in those places); the places that can be reached on foot, or by public or private transport (in the time-frame available to the user); and the virtual places and people that can be reached through computer networks.

Coffee Shops, Libraries, and Co-Working Spaces as Temporary and Hybrid Workplaces

A variety of concepts have permeated much of the current research on temporary and hybrid workplaces. Terms such as satellite office, guest office, instant office, and home office, have been associated with the ongoing concept of flexible work and related spatial requirements of organizations, as well as freelancers (Vartianinen et al., 2007). People work in so-called "hybrid workplaces," which are in-between homes, organizations, and virtual spaces (Vartiainen and Hyrkkänen, 2010). Additionally, it has been argued that each generation of workers has a specific workplace, related expectations, and spatial requirements (Haynes, 2011). For example, the newest entrants to the workplaces, the so-called generation Y or Millennials – those born between 1981 and 2000 – tend to use technology as an integral part of their everyday lives. The Millennials see the office as an extension of their home life and are increasingly mobile. "They are transforming both social behavior and the way that business is undertaken" (Haynes, 2011: 101).

In the eighteenth century in Europe, coffeehouses represented one of the institutions of civil society. Coffeehouses were not only places where a cup of coffee could be enjoyed, but they were also havens for reading and discussion (Meinel and Sack, 2014). The coffeehouse, including clubs, used to represent literal and symbolic sites of the bourgeois class. During those periods, private individuals from the educated middle class started participating in the life of civil society (Habermas, 1989: 29). Merchants, bankers, entrepreneurs, and manufacturers used to conduct their business in coffeehouses, while writers, artists, and scientists used to meet there to read, exchange news, and hold discussions (Meinel and Sack, 2014). In contrast with the past, coffee shops have changed their roles and functions during the Information Age. This has happened for several reasons, such as the changes of individual habits and the new ways of communicating and working (e.g., by e-mail and via Skype), as well as the provision of new services and facilities that can be found in coffee shops (such as Wi-Fi and meeting rooms). Brown and O'Hara (2003) called coffee shops "semi-offices." This function is possible, even though work-related activities and conversation might be disturbed by the noise, lighting conditions, and spatial features—which are not designed as in offices (Sanusi and Palen, 2008). Referring to Friebe and Lobo (2006), Hartmann (2009) described the particular group of customers that choose coffee shops for working as so-called "digital Bohemians." These Bohemians, who are mostly artists and web designers, seem to lead a "new working life style," in which the "borders between work and free time might be challenged" (Hartmann, 2009: 432). However, there is little research on the actual reasons that people choose coffee shops as temporary places to work.

Public libraries have a long history as learning spaces (Houghton et al., 2013), but users have recently also used the library as a place to meet friends, classmates, and colleagues (May and Black, 2010; Aabø and Audunson, 2012). Libraries are thus challenging the traditional concept of learning space by including a range of new functions, such as listening to music, printing, and video editing, as well as meeting friends and colleagues. In addition, several facilities and new elements of interior design have been introduced, such as lounge areas, couches, meeting rooms, whiteboards, projectors, video consoles, and coffee and food bars (Bilandzic and Foth, 2013). To this end, the State Library of Queensland (SLQ) has recently provided a co-working space that is called "The Edge" and is meant to be a place to discuss new projects of digital technology. Bilandzic and Foth (2013) observed and interviewed people who usually share this co-working space and discuss their own creative ideas. The study was mostly addressed at understanding whether socio-spatial and technological aspects of libraries facilitate social learning between the library users. Only a few recent studies have focused on the physical features of libraries that provide informal and temporary working spaces, such as the Openbare Bibliotheek van Amsterdam (Servet, 2010).

Furthermore, co-working spaces are proliferating around the world. According to Johns and Gratton (2013), there were more than 2,000 co-working spaces around the globe, and there has been an increase of 250 percent over two years. Freelancers and small start-ups mostly use co-working spaces that are multipurpose spaces in an informal working environment (Spinuzzi, 2012; Gandini, 2015; Lee, 2016). A growing number of organizations are adopting non-traditional workplace policies and design strategies for creative working environments (Lee, 2016).

Co-working spaces have applied the design of a fun and whimsical ambience of a coffee shop in this context (Lee, 2016). These spaces provide more than a table or a free Internet connection. In fact, the spatial characteristics and locations of places as well as the "low entry barriers" are extremely important for creative individuals (Florida, 2002). Referring to Messina, Moriset (2014) argued that the core principle of co-working spaces is the possibility of increasing fruitful encounters. In addition to large technology corporations, policymakers and city planners have recently recognized the relevance of co-working spaces (Moriset, 2014). For these reasons, some co-working spaces have lately received public support. However, little is known about free-of-charge spaces that have been completely sponsored by municipal governments and by other public institutions, such as universities.

The Context of Finland

Since the 1990s, telework in Finland has been considered a new way of arranging work and creating "win-win situations" for employers and employees (Luukinen et al., 1996). By framing the Finnish context, Puro (2002) argued that mobile phones contribute to changing the attitudes of those who do not clearly distinguish between a private call and a "work-oriented" one and, consequently, work and private life have become increasingly mixed.

According to the latest *Statistics*, 90 percent of the Finnish population currently has access to an Internet connection at home, while 68 percent use the Internet several times a day. In 2015, almost 30 percent of the population used the web with tablets outside home and workplace, while 62 percent of Finns had accessed it with a mobile phone (Statistics Finland, 2015). Furthermore, according to the latest European Working Conditions Survey, Finland has the highest percentage of employees involved in telework (Eurofound, 2012). In particular, 45 percent of Finnish workers can work remotely away from the office or from the main place of work. The findings from Eurofound survey show that most of the teleworkers are highly qualified men who work full time with flexible contracts (65 percent). They are mostly engaged in the sectors of financial services, education, public administration, and defense.

Furthermore, the metropolitan areas of Helsinki, Tampere, and Oulu have recently seen an increasing proliferation of both private and public co-working spaces. Referring in particular to the metropolitan area of Helsinki, public co-working spaces are located in the Helsinki city center, as well as in the northeastern peripheral district of Viikki, and Otaniemi, one of the districts in the neighboring municipality of Espoo. Co-working spaces are located within the two campuses of Otaniemi and Viikki, in which Aalto University and the University of Helsinki are situated, respectively (See Figure 1). The University of Helsinki also has a central campus in the city center and Kumpula, respectively. Helsinki Think Company, for instance, provides co-working and event spaces both in the city center and the Viikki Campus. Helsinki Think Company is sponsored by both the University of Helsinki and the City of Helsinki. Most of the paid co-working spaces, such as HUB13, Kontoret, Deck, and Magasinet Creative Hub are centrally located, as well as Regus. Regus manages co-working spaces for rent in several central neighborhoods, such as Töölönlahti and Punavuori, as well as Pasila. Paid co-working spaces, such as Mainio Social and Software Factory, can be found in Otaniemi and the Kumpula Campus, respectively. In addition, a so-called urban office is provided by Kallio Library (See Figure 1). The concept of urban office has its origin in the strategy of Helsinki City Library. An urban office provides both quiet working zones and lobby spaces for meetings or conversation via Skype and telephone (City of Helsinki, 2012). Urban offices have been designed in the new Helsinki Central Library, which is currently under construction in the Töölönlahti area, the cultural neighborhood of the City of Helsinki.

Furthermore, the City of Helsinki is developing urban policies to support co-working spaces. In the new Master Plan, in particular in Vision 2050, the City of Helsinki has recognized the necessity of providing an urban structure that enables space for new creative thinking and new technologies. "We need more spaces in which people meet, enjoy themselves and engage in recreational activities, and in which there are incentives to

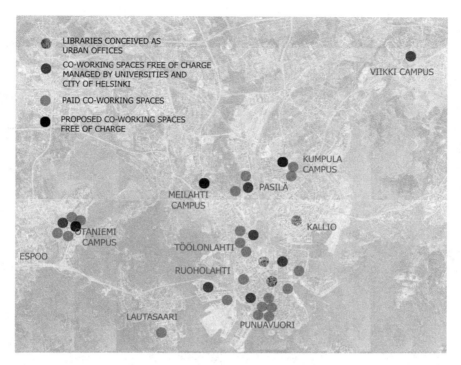

Figure 1: Free of charge and paid co-working spaces and libraries conceived as urban offices in the Metropolitan Area of Helsinki

work and be an entrepreneur" (Helsinki City, 2013: 6). However, by analyzing the other official documents, one can find little evidence of plans that could support the mentioned vision. The City of Helsinki has prioritized the provision of WLAN-services for residents and travelers. Thus far, the WLAN service is offered in the large urban area that covers the city center and one of the main ring roads (Kehä I), as well as along the main arteries of Länsiväylä and Itäväylä, and the railway tracks (See Figure 2). People can access outdoor and indoor hotspots for free and without the need for a password or registration. In addition to the public Wi-Fi spots, several commercial services offer free Internet access, especially within the inner city.

Methodology

The research methods included conducting qualitative (structured and semi-structured) interviews and observing teleworkers in Café Köket, Meetingpoint, and Helsinki Think Company.

Café Köket and Meetingpoint are part of a larger research project that aimed to investigate flexible working and living in the Metropolitan Area of Helsinki. We observed 10 public and semi-public spaces, including public and university libraries, coffee shops, parks, gardens, and squares that are located in the Helsinki city center. The observations were conducted for 105 hours. In addition, 150 semi-structured interviews were conducted with the people who used those places to work. This

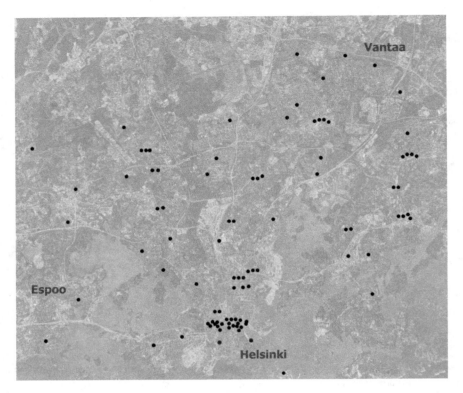

Figure 2: Geographical distribution of free outdoor and indoor hotspots within the Metropolitan Area of Helsinki

study also included Helsinki Think Company, which was added to the larger research project.

The reasons for selecting Café Köket, Meetingpoint, and Helsinki Think Company are that they challenge the traditional concept of the workplace. Increasing attention is paid to these alternative workplaces among scholars and politicians, as well as the managers of the places themselves. In particular, the urban policies of public libraries in Helsinki are intentionally challenging the traditional concept of library (in terms of buildings and functions) by providing spaces and services for different activities, such as working. Café Köket provides facilities, such as Wi-Fi spots and meeting rooms for additional activities (e.g., meeting with colleagues and clients). Helsinki Think Company has been added as a case study which considers the new spaces, facilities, and virtual services that only a few co-working spaces in Europe have been recently proposing as free to use. The Company offers all the same equipment of an office (such as Wi-Fi, coffee, whiteboards, and markers). The design has also kept in mind new temporary and hybrid working practices.

In order to find suitable interviewees, the people who were using IT devices were approached by asking specifically if they were working, and if they would be willing to participate in the research project. Since it was assumed that workers are usually busy with their own work, the interviews were kept brief, no longer than 10 minutes. The number of respondents in Café Köket, Meetingpoint, and Helsinki Think Company were 31, 30, and 17, respectively. Furthermore, the directors of Café Köket, Meetingpoint, and Helsinki

Think Company were also interviewed. The questions dealt with several topics, such as ways of supporting formal and informal co-working spaces around the city, and the kind of urban policies and practices that should be adopted.

Seventeen visits in total were carried out to the three places for a total of 54 hours, and 78 teleworkers were interviewed. Each visit took between one and five hours, with the average visit being approximately three hours. The spatial characteristics of the three spaces were analyzed, including location and connections. Observations and interviews were carried out from 8.30am to 12pm in the mornings and 12pm to 6pm in the afternoons from June to October 2013, excluding July, the summer holiday month in Finland. Helsinki Think Company was observed later, in September and October 2015.

The surrounding urban structure and services were also scrutinized, and the architectural and spatial attributes of each place were evaluated. To this end, the accessibility from surrounding neighborhoods was investigated, including the availability of public transportation and pedestrian and cycling connections. The nearby functions were also examined in order to understand the urban fabric that characterizes the context of the three places. The inside and outside physical features of the three places were also observed. The study used an architectural features checklist to frame the three places, supported by comprehensive visual documentation.

The structured and semi-structured interviews were conducted with the aim of understanding the reasons people choose these places to work (See Appendix). In order to profile the respondents, the study first focused on exploring the demographic, educational, and employment characteristics of the interviewed teleworkers (e.g., sex, age, level of education, field of primary occupation, type of contract, and main workplace). Second, semi-structured interviews consisting of 12 questions were led to explore the workers' routines and habits (See Appendix). The respondents, for example, were asked about the length of time they usually spent in that place to work and their reasons for choosing it as a place to work. They were also asked about their personal preferences for the spaces, considering the spatial features. In addition, they were questioned about which other workplaces they had used before reaching the coffee shop, the urban office, or the co-working space. Since this was a qualitative study of three cases, the results naturally cannot be generalized to all coffee shops, urban offices, and co-working spaces, but they can be used to characterize typical habits of workers in such central locations and related socio-spatial features of those places.

Findings

Spatial Characteristics of Café Köket, Meetingpoint, and Helsinki Think Company

Figure 3 shows that Café Köket, Meetingpoint, and the Helsinki Think Company are surrounded by a mixed range of services, offices, and housing. The urban spaces around the three places are designed more for pedestrians than vehicular traffic. To this end, a comprehensive and connected network of parks, gardens, and squares around Café Köket, Meetingpoint, and Helsinki Think Company is easily accessible by bicycle and on foot. Rail commuters can easily arrive at the heart of the city, since the Central Railway Station offers rapid connections between the central areas and other parts of Helsinki. In addition, commuters and other passengers can approach by sea via the South

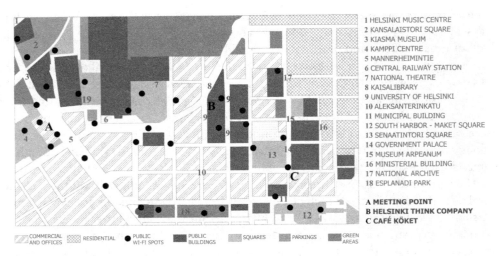

Figure 3: Urban functions in the City Center of Helsinki and spatial distribution of public Wi-Fi spots

Harbor. Furthermore, a large number of indoor and outdoor spaces in the city center offer wireless access; Helsinki City open WLAN, which is managed by the IT department of the City of Helsinki, is free. The open network stretches from the Kamppi Center to the Railway Station, as well as from the Esplanadi Park to the Senate Square. The open WLAN is sufficiently fast to enable video calls and a rapid check of e-mail and calendars.

In particular, Café Köket is located in the historic center of Helsinki. During the research project, the coffee shop was located on the ground floor of a building that opened partially onto Senaatintori Square, facing Aleksanterinkatu, one of the main commercial streets of Helsinki. Subsequently, it moved to one of the neighboring blocks. It could be easily reached by tram and on foot from the Central Railway Station and from the nearby metro stations. It was relatively close to the University of Helsinki as well as several state and municipal buildings. In addition to food, drinks, and comfortable and well-designed spaces, the coffee shop provided a meeting room that could be booked by clients.

Meetingpoint, which faced one of the main commercial streets, Mannerheimintie, was located on the first floor of the Lasipalatsi Building (the Glass Palace). At the time of writing, the building is under renovation, and the activities will be moved to the new Helsinki Central Library. The Glass Palace is a five-minute walk from Kamppi, which is the major transport hub and shopping center of the City. The urban office is surrounded by retail and office functions, while it is around five minutes on foot from various cultural buildings and public spaces, such as Kiasma, the Museum of Contemporary Art; the Helsinki Music Centre; and the nearby Kansalaistori Square (See Figure 3). As previously mentioned, Meetingpoint was unusual as a "library," since it did not have a book collection; rather, it provided additional and innovative services, such as practical advice and guidance on video editing and software. Due to its informal meeting rooms and individual seats that could be booked online for working, Meetingpoint was called an "urban office."

Helsinki Think Company is located beside the main library of the University of Helsinki, Kaisa Library. The building has been transformed from commercial use. The spacious rooms characterized by large windows are currently provided free of charge as co-working spaces. It is only a five-minute walk from the Central Railway Station. It is easy to reach the Senate Square and surroundings from Helsinki Think Company, where several departments of the University of Helsinki and Government buildings are located. The co-working space is on the ground floor and visible from outside through three huge windows that face the Kaisaniemi Metro Station.

The Reasons for Working in Café Köket, Meetingpoint, and Helsinki Think Company

Based on the interviews, the aim was to identify the main reasons teleworkers choose Café Köket, Meetingpoint, and Helsinki Think Company as places to work. The teleworkers have different habits, needs, and spatial requirements, and this might be related, for instance, to the fields of primary occupation. The teleworkers in Café Köket are mostly engaged in business and finance, social services, and government, as well as education and research and information technology. The urban office of Meetingpoint seems to attract more people who are involved in the fields of arts and culture, and business and finances, and less those who are engaged in information technology. Helsinki Think Company is mostly preferred by those workers who are employed in the sectors of business and finance, and information technology (See Table 1).

The other occupations that have been found in the Meetingpoint are weakly represented, such as the fields of education and research, information technology, and social services and government. A few teleworkers who were interviewed in Helsinki Think Company were involved in the fields of arts and culture, human resources, sales and services, and communication (See Table 1).

The youngest teleworkers (between 18 and 24 years) were found mostly in Helsinki Think Company. Respondents between 25 and 34 years old used to work in all three places, whereas respondents between 35 and 64 years old were found only in Café Köket and Meetingpoint. Furthermore, those employed by large organizations and entrepreneurs chose Café Köket as their place to work. Entrepreneurs and those employed by small organizations were found in Helsinki Think Company, while entrepreneurs and freelancers preferred working in Meetingpoint (See Table 2).

There was a considerable presence of women in the coffee shop, while Meetingpoint and Helsinki Think Company seemed to be more attractive to male teleworkers. One of the reasons is that in Café Köket a large number of teleworkers interviewed were employed in the fields of social services and government (See Table 1) that have more female employees than other fields.

Table 1: Fields of primary occupation, Café Köket, Meetingpoint, and Helsinki Think Company

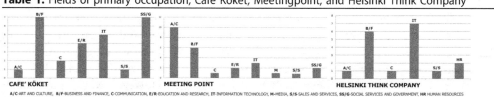

A/C-ART AND CULTURE, B/F-BUSINESS AND FINANCE, C-COMMUNICATION, E/R-EDUCATION AND RESEARCH, IT-INFORMATION TECHNOLOGY, M-MEDIA, S/S-SALES AND SERVICES, SS/G-SOCIAL SERVICES AND GOVERNMENT, HR HUMAN RESOURCES

Table 2: Type of contracts Café Köket, Meetingpoint, and Helsinki Think Company (F-freelancer, E-entrepreneur, ESO-employed by a small organization, EMO-employed by a medium organization, ELO-employed by a large organization)

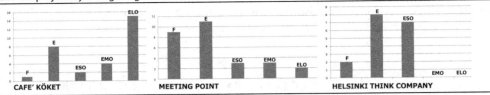

One of the main reasons to use Café Köket, Meetingpoint, and Helsinki Think Company is the easy accessibility by public transportation and the central location. Workers use these spaces because they are close to their clients' premises, offices, and homes. To this end, a worker interviewed in Cafe' Köket described it as follows:

> My main workplace is the office. Usually I work here once or twice a week for one hour. The best feature of this place is the location since the coffee shop is close to home and my clients' premises. I am leaving in 15 minutes because of a meeting with my clients.

It might be assumed that there are teleworkers who come from the surrounding offices, since there are several ministerial and municipal buildings around Café Köket. They appreciate the good breakfast or having lunch while meeting colleagues. However, people also choose to meet colleagues and clients in Café Köket or work alone at all sorts of time of the day beyond the traditional meal times of breakfast or lunch. Moreover, the nearby services represent a relevant reason for choosing these spaces for working. A worker interviewed in Helsinki Think Company said that:

> My main workplace is home; however, I come here once a week for 6–7 hours and usually I have meetings with my colleagues. It is easy to reach Helsinki Think Company by public transportation, and afterwards I go habitually to buy groceries from around here.

Unlike Meetingpoint and Café Köket, Helsinki Think Company represents a place to network with other entrepreneurs. There are business related events that are periodically organized and people arrive with new business ideas to share. A common feature between respondents interviewed in Helsinki Think Company and Meetingpoint is the difficulty of finding affordable office space to rent in the city center. Therefore, the free access to the space, including Wi-Fi and meeting rooms are relevant aspects for workers. A respondent at Meetingpoint said that:

> I choose several places to work, such as home, offices, coffee shops, and libraries. Usually I come here in the morning and once a week for 2–4 hours. I like this place because of the free access, good Wi-Fi, and public transportation.

What teleworkers of Café Köket, Meetingpoint, and Helsinki Think Company have in common is that they frequently move around the urban spaces of the city (such as coffee shops, libraries, and co-working spaces) using them as temporary workplaces. This happens because of the need to work in-between meetings and to commute long distances from suburban workplaces to the city center. Changing the scenario from their daily workplace also represents an important reason among the teleworkers, and, thus, they search for a working environment that they actually like. However, working out of the office can simply mean looking for comfortable places that offer extra services, such as a good breakfast and lunch, or free Wi-Fi. This is particularly true of the teleworkers in Café Köket. In addition, quiet as well as natural and good lighting attract the teleworkers in Meetingpoint.

The respondents were asked which other places they had visited before arriving at Café Köket, Meetingpoint, and Helsinki Think Company. The network of public, semi-public, and private spaces that the respondents in Café Köket described is composed of home, office, coffee shops, and clients' premises. Once arrived at the coffee shop, teleworkers have usually already worked in some of those places and even on the bus. The network of urban spaces used by entrepreneurs and freelancers who frequently visit Meetingpoint is larger and includes libraries, trains, pubs, co-working spaces, and lounge areas of hotels. Entrepreneurs and those employed by small organizations, who were interviewed in Helsinki Think Company, do not choose libraries as workplaces, but mostly other co-working spaces in the city center and also the Viikki Campus.

The teleworkers in Café Köket work in the coffee shop from one to two hours per week, but sometimes for shorter periods (e.g., 30 minutes once a week), while people spend a longer time (at least three hours) in Meetingpoint and Helsinki Think Company. It can be assumed that, since most of the teleworkers interviewed in Café Köket are employed by large organizations, their work contracts are not flexible enough to allow them to work for prolonged time out of the office. However, it is also reasonable to assume that this is related to the fact that the coffee shop is a private business, and its business model is usually based on selling beverages and food, not on renting space that is occupied. Although it is clear that those who try to spend time without buying anything are asked to leave, there are no clear rules as to how much one is supposed to consume if one spends several hours occupying a coffee table. Thus, it is natural that coffee shops are used as more temporary locations than libraries and co-working spaces, for instance, and therefore workers from the surrounding offices mostly use them.

Furthermore, the managers of the three places talked about urban policies and practices that should be developed in order to adapt the city to new emerging working practices. The manager of Café Köket painted an interesting picture of the city center when she mentioned:

> The central business district does not provide any informal places to work. Teleworkers struggle to find places in which it is possible to print and find spacious places for meetings. In addition to private investors, the City of Helsinki might support the opening of spaces to work by converting several buildings to multiple functions. This can happen in partnership with the private sector. The coffeehouse can be located in several premises. It would be interesting to find a new way to mix urban functions.

The director of Meetingpoint confirmed that the model of the urban office will be exported to the new Helsinki Central Library. In the new project, new spaces that are dedicated to working will be designed on the second floor. Furthermore, one of the directors of Helsinki Think Company presents another picture about co-working spaces:

> Based on my understanding, there are not so many co-working spaces in Helsinki. The most popular ones are Helsinki Think Company and HUB 13. The City and the University want to help young entrepreneurs to start their own businesses. It would be nice to ask politicians to visit these kinds of co-working spaces and discuss our current and future needs (such as more and bigger spaces). On the other hand, one of the priorities would be to contact companies that are interested in networking with the young entrepreneurs of Helsinki Think Company.

> With this in mind, the co-working space of Startup Sauna in Otaniemi should be taken as an example. In my opinion, libraries are not co-working spaces, but co-working spaces can easily replace coffee shops as workplaces.

It is evident that semi-public spaces, such as coffee shops, are still re-thinking their business models and layout, just as public spaces, including public libraries, are renewing services and facilities. On the other hand, based on the interview with the director of Helsinki Think Company, one can see that there is not a complete awareness of the proliferation of co-working spaces within the Metropolitan Region of Helsinki. In addition, there is still a tendency to exclude libraries from emerging workplaces and to believe that co-working spaces can replace coffee shops.

Discussion

The findings show that coffee shops, urban offices of libraries, and co-working spaces have become natural alternatives to traditional working locations, and mostly for those engaged in specific occupations. Contrary to what might be assumed, and based on the main findings from previous studies, teleworkers in Café Köket are mostly engaged in business and finance, social services and government and information technology, while the number of artists and writers who work there is not significant. On the other hand, the teleworkers interviewed in Meetingpoint are mainly involved in art and culture and less in business and finance. In Helsinki Think Company, the workers are engaged in the fields of information technology and business and finance. Therefore, in a way, one can say that the bourgeoisie (or rather, upper middle class) has dominated the coffee shops, and they have also discovered the co-working spaces as spaces for work, while the most precarious workers have chosen the urban office (See Table 2).

This paper aims to contribute to the current knowledge of emerging workplaces. In addition to ICT infrastructures, socio-spatial characteristics affect the choice of these emerging workplaces. People cannot easily work everywhere because the networks are not everywhere (or equally fast or free of charge) as we saw in the Metropolitan Area of Helsinki. On the other hand, physical spaces still matter for several reasons. In fact, the differences in clientele are connected, for instance, to the location of places, easy access, and means of transport. Based on the findings from the interviews, we might claim that networking different workplaces, such as co-working spaces, libraries, coffee shops, home, and office, as well as rearranging time and space, might be a necessity or a way to escape from routine. This means that the typical office environment does not completely meet the workers' needs. However, one can also add that working in multiple places––public and semi-public––is simply related to the fact that new working practices do not require a stable office, but places to work temporarily, individually, or as a group, or network with clients and other start-ups.

The study points out that working in public and semi-public spaces is still dealing with cultural and social obstacles and differences in the type of telework and field of occupation. Working in public spaces (such as libraries and co-working spaces) or semi-public spaces (such as coffee shops) seems to provide a specific working network, new knowledge, or simply productivity and concentration. On the other hand, escaping from the office (and thus not being seen, and not communicating face-to-face) may be challenging for workers due to their employment contracts and their particular occupations.

Information and communication technologies combined with the growing flexibility of work are contributing to reshaping the way we experience public and semi-public spaces (Vartiainen and Hyrkkänen, 2010; Koroma et al., 2014). These phenomena have been studied mainly in the fields of organizational studies, business, and management, while this study aims to add a socio-spatial perspective when exploring emerging workplaces. The physical boundaries, norms, and behaviors shape the ways in which we use public and semi-public spaces. (Madanipour, 2003). However, the study points out that activities that have never been planned before within public and semi-public spaces are emerging and shaping new socio-spatial relationships. This also means that physical and virtual boundaries should both be kept in mind in a systematic view when exploring public and semi-public spaces.

Since this research was based mainly on qualitative interviews and three case studies, it naturally cannot be generalized from the results that the workers detected in the coffee shop, the library conceived as an urban office, and the co-working space would represent all users of these kinds of premises. Nevertheless, the results also contribute to an understanding of the increasing urban network of commuting workers (Nael, 2013). The findings also contribute to an understanding of the flow of commuting workers that can enlarge the concept of commuting residents (Davoudi and Madanipour, 2012; Tummers and Zibell, 2012). Temporary and commuting residents can own or rent a second home in the cities, but they can also be the ones who commute daily for working reasons and use urban spaces temporarily.

In addition to this, the study suggested that different users choose and appropriate their temporary workplaces for their specific purposes. In fact, these places are freely chosen by their users for working purposes; thus, our study represents a bottom-up approach to understanding multi-functionality in contemporary urban spaces. This user-driven perspective in planning and design is often emphasized in theory and practice, but it is still challenging to step from functionalistic spatial divisions to overlapping fields of changing and multifunctional spaces of post-functionalist cities. The study underlines that mixed use and changing activities can be found in diverse places such as libraries and coffee shops. This is also based on the new strategies being addressed by directors of libraries and coffee shops. Furthermore, this emerging approach of converting buildings into new and multiple functions, such as co-working spaces (both free and paid), represents an attempt to add flexibility and the opening of possibilities which cities, investors and policymakers are struggling to provide.

In fact, this study points out that there is a call for a post-functionalist city, in which there is a need to go beyond the functionalist division of spaces and services. This is already happening when one can find public libraries conceived as urban offices, as well as free co-working spaces. This approach goes beyond the current perspective of public services, in which, for instance, libraries are not always understood as an investment, but mostly as public spending, in local politics. Paid co-working spaces have been seen recently as incubators of new start-ups, but mainly from the point of view of the high-tech fields. However, municipal governments and universities still need to understand that public support for co-working spaces might be relevant to generate new business opportunities, as well as new knowledge and innovation. This approach might also help to revise the concept of public services within the urban policies and practices of post-functionalist cities.

Conclusions

The study revealed that working in multiple places, especially public and semi-public spaces, is not an urban myth, but is actually happening and changing the way spaces are appropriated and used for different purposes.

The aim of the study was to present the socio-spatial characteristics of emerging workplaces within the city. The study also revealed ways and reasons people appropriate public and semi-public spaces for their own working purposes. The proliferation of non-traditional workplaces, such as libraries, coffee shops, and co-working spaces, has to be further investigated within urban policies and practices, considering not only the socio-spatial characteristics of those urban spaces, but also the growth of ICTs, the growing flexibility of work, as well as the tendency to work and live in multiple places.

Moreover, it is equally evident that the planning and designing of these spaces is lagging behind, although many cities have innovative policies to promote Internet connections in public spaces, as well as new functions for public services. The functionalist understanding of public and private spaces is still clearly one of the obstacles to accommodating new and flexible functions in these spaces. Co-working spaces, coffee shops, and libraries have been transformed into emerging workplaces, although this phenomenon needs to be further interpreted according to the changing of spatial and time-settings, as well as the personal preferences of teleworkers. Flexibility and the emerging possibilities of post-functionalist cities need to be further explored by policymakers, investors, and experts, such as planners and architects.

Acknowledgments

We are grateful to Arla Joensuu, Kari Lämsa, and Henri Virta, who are directors of Cafe' Köket, Meetingpoint, and Helsinki Think Company, respectively, for providing their insights during the interviews.

Funding

The project was conducted at Aalto University and supported by Tekes (The Finnish Funding Agency for Innovation) in partnership with Telia Sonera, Café Köket, Regus and Helsinki City Library, under a grant (number 40277/12).

Bibliography

S. Aabø and R. Audunson, "Use of Library Space and the Library as Place," *Library & Information Science Research* 34 (2012) 138–149.

K. Al-Kodmany, "Sentient City: Ubiquitous Computing, Architecture, and the Future of Urban Space," *Journal of Urban Technology* 19: 3 (2012) 137–140.

T. Banerjee, "The Future of Public Space: Beyond Invented Streets and Reinvented Places," *Journal of the American Planning Association* 67: 1 (2001) 9–24.

F. Bar and N. Park, "Municipal Wi-Fi: the Goals, Practices, and Policy Implications of the U.S. Case," *Communications & Strategies* 61: 1st quarter (2006) 107–125.

M. Batty, E. Besussi, K. Maat, and J.J. Harts, "Representing Multifunctional Cities: Density and Diversity in Space and Time," *Built Environment* 30: 4 (2004) 324–337.

M. Bilandzic and M. Foth, "Libraries as Co-working Spaces: Understanding User Motivations and Perceived Barriers to Social Learning," *Library Hi Tech* 31: 2 (2013) 254–273.

B. Brown and K. O'Hara, "Place as a Practical Concern of Mobile Workers," *Environment and Planning A* 35: 9 (2003) 1565–1587.

M. Carmona, *Public Places, Urban Spaces: The Dimensions of Urban Design* (London: Architectural Press, 2003).

M. Carmona, "Re-theorising Contemporary Public Space: a New Narrative and a New Normative," *Journal of Urbanism: International Research on Place Making and Urban Sustainability* 8: 4 (2015) 373–405.

M. Castells, *The Rise of the Network Society: The Information Age: Economy, Society, and Culture*, Volume 1 (Oxford: Wiley & Backwell, Second Edition, 2011).

City of Helsinki, *The Heart of the Metropolis-Helsinki Central Library Architectural Competition 2017. Helsinki, Finland: Central Library* (Helsinki: City of Helsinki, 2012) <http://competition.keskustakirjasto.fi/> Accessed September 20, 2016.

S. Davoudi and A. Madanipour, "Two Charters of Athens and Two Visions of Utopia: Functional and Connected," *Built Environment* 38: 4 (2012) 459–468.

Eurofound, *Trends in Job Quality in Europe* (Luxembourg: European Union, 2012). <http://eurofound.europa.eu/sites/default/files/ef_files/pubdocs/2012/28/en/1/EF1228EN.pdf> Accessed October 9, 2016.

A.M. Fernandez-Maldonado, "ICT and Spatial Planning in European Cities: Reviewing the New Charter of Athens," *Built Environment* 38: 4 (2012) 469–483.

R. Florida, *The Rise of the Creative Class. And How It's Transforming Work, Leisure and Everyday Life* (New York: Basic Books, 2002).

L. Forlano, "Mobile Lifestyles in the Business World," *The International Encyclopedia of Digital Communication and Society* (2015). doi:10.1002/9781118767771.wbiedcs091

M. Foth and P. Sanders, "Impacts of Social Computing on the Architecture of Urban Spaces," in A. Aurigi and F. De Cindio, ed., *Augmented Urban Spaces* (Abingdon, Oxon, GBR: Ashgate Publishing Group, 2008) 73–92.

H. Friebe and S. Lobo, *Wir nennen es Arbeit: Die Digitale Boheme oder: Intelligentes Leben jenseits der Festanstellung* (München: Heyne, 2006).

S. Ganapati and C.F. Shoepp, "The Wireless City," *International Journal of Electronic Government Research*, 4: 4 (2008) 54–68.

A. Gandini, "The Rise of Co-Working Spaces: A Literature Review," *Ephemera, Theories and Politics in Organizations* 15: 1 (2015) 193–205. <http://www.ephemerajournal.org/contribution/rise-coworking-spaces-literature-review> Accessed September 19, 2016.

J. Gehl, *Life Between Buildings. Using Public Space* (London: Island Press, 2011).

T. Grubesic and A. Murray, ""Where" Matters: Location and Wi-Fi Access," *Journal of Urban Technology* 11: 1 (2004) 1–28.

J. Habermas, *The Structural Transformation of the Public Sphere* (Cambridge MA: Polity Press, 1989).

S. Halford, "Hybrid Workspace: Re-spatialisations of Work, Organisation and Management," *New Technology, Work and Employment*, 20: 1 (2005) 19–33.

K.N. Hampton, "Community and Social Interaction in the Wireless City: Wi-Fi Use in Public and Semi-Public Spaces," *New Media & Society* 10: 6 (2008) 831–850.

K.N. Hampton, O. Livio and L. Sessions Goulet, "The Social Life of Wireless Urban, Spaces: Internet Use, Social Networks, and the Public Realm," *Journal of Communication* 60: 4 (2010) 701–722.

M. Hartmann, "The Changing Urban Landscapes of Media Consumption and Production," *European Journal of Communication* 24: 4 (2009) 421–436.

B.P. Haynes, "The Impact of Generational Differences on the Workplace," *Journal of Corporate Real Estate* 13: 2 (2011) 98–108. <https://doi.org/10.1108/14630011111136812> Accessed September 20, 2016.

Helsinki City, *Vision 2050, Urban Plan - The New Helsinki City Plan* (2013). <http://www.hel.fi/hel2/ksv/julkaisut/yos_2013-23_en.pdf> Accessed October 3, 2016.

K. Houghton, M. Foth and E. Miller, "The Continuing Relevance of the Library as a Third Place for Users and Non-users of IT: the Case of Canada Bay," *The Australian Library Journal* 62: 1 (2013) 27–39.

T. Johns and L. Gratton, *Spotlight on the Future of Knowledge Work. The Third Wave of Virtual Work. Knowledge Workers are Now Untethered, Able to Perform Tasks Anywhere at any Time. What do the Best of them Want From Your Organization?* (Harvard: Business School Publishing, 2013) <http://www.harvardbusiness.org/sites/default/files/HBR_Third_Wave_of_Virtual_Work.pdf> Accessed October 19, 2016.

J. Koroma, U. Hyrkkänen, and M. Vartiainen, "Looking for People, Places and Connections: Hindrances when Working in Multiple Locations: a Review," *New Technology, Work and Employment* 29: 2 (2014) 139–159.

K. Lapintie, "Modalities of Urban Space," *Planning Theory* 6: 1 (2007) 36–51.

Y.S. Lee, "Creative Workplace Characteristics and Innovative Start-up Companies," *Facilities* 34: 7/8 (2016) 413–432.

L. Lofland, *A World of Strangers: Order and Action in Urban Public Spaces* (New York: Basic Books, 1973).

A. Luukinen, J. Pekkola and R. Suomi, "Telework Arrangements Demand in Finland," paper presented at the 29th Annual Hawaii International Conference on System Sciences (1996) <https://www.computer.org/csdl/proceedings/hicss/1996/7330/00/73300366.pdf> Accessed September 15, 2016.

A. Madanipour, *Public and Private Spaces of the City* (London: Routledge, 2003).

F. May and F. Black, "The Life of the Space: Evidence from Nova Scotia Public Libraries," *Evidence Based Library and Information Practice* 5: 2 (2010) 5–34.

V. Mehta, "Evaluating Public Space," *Journal of Urban Design* 19 (2014) 53–88.

C. Meinel and H. Sack, *Digital Communication, X. Media. Publishing* (Berlin Heidelberg: Springer-Verlag, 2014).

B. Moriset, "Building New Places of the Creative Economy. The Rise of Co-working Spaces," paper presented at the 2nd Geography of Innovation International Conference (Utrecht, January 23 January 25, 2014) <https://halshs.archives-ouvertes.fr/halshs-00914075> Accessed September 13, 2016.

Z.P. Nael, *The Connected City: How Networks Are Shaping the Modern Metropolis* (New York: Routledge, 2013).

R. Oldenburg, *The Great Good Place: Cafés, Coffee Shops, Nookstores, Bars, Hair Salons, and other Hangouts at the Heart of a Community* (New York, NY: Marlowe & Company, 1999).

R. Oldenburg, *Celebrating the Third Place: Inspiring Stories about the "Great Good Places" at the Heart of Our Communities* (New York, NY: Marlowe & Company, 2001).

J.P. Puro, "Finland: a Mobile Culture," in J.E. Katz and M. Aakhus, ed., *Perpetual Contact Mobile Communication, Private Talk, Public Performance* (Cambridge: University Press, 2002) 19–29.

P. Pyöriä, "Knowledge Work in Distributed Environments: Issues and Illusions," *New Technology, Work and Employment* 18: 3 (2003) 166–180.

A. Sanusi and L. Palen, "Of Coffee Shops and Parking Lots: Considering Matters of Space and Place in the Use of Public Wi-Fi," *Computer Supported Cooperative Work* 17: 2 (2008) 257–273.

T. Schwanen and M.-P. Kwan, "The Internet, Mobile Phone and Space-Time Constraints," *Journal Geoforum* 39: 3 (2008) 1362–1377.

M. Servet, "Les Bibliothèques Troisième Lieu, une Nouvelle Génération d'Établissements Culturels," (2010) <http://bbf.enssib.fr/consulter/bbf-2010-04-0057-001> Accessed November 3, 2015.

C. Spinuzzi, "Working Alone Together. Coworking as Emergent Collaborative Activity," *Journal of Business and Technical Communication* 26: 4 (2012) 399–441.

Statistics Finland. 2015. <http://www.stat.fi/til/sutivi/2015/sutivi_2015_2015-11-26_tie_001_en.html> Accessed October 13, 2016.

A.M. Townsend, "Life in the Real-Time City: Mobile Telephones and Urban Metabolism," *Journal of Urban Technology* 7: 2 (2000) 85–104.

L. Tummers and B. Zibell, "What Can Spatial Planners Do to Create the 'Connected City'? A Gendered Reading of the Charters of Athens," *Built Environment* 38: 4 (2012) 524–539.

M. Vartiainen and U. Hyrkkänen, "Changing Requirements and Mental Workload Factors in Mobile, Multi-locational Work," *New Technology, Work and Employment* 25: 2 (2010) 117–135.

M. Vartiainen, M. Hakonen, P. Mannonen, M.P. Nieminen, V. Ruohomäki and A. Vartola, *Distributed and Mobile Work – Places, People and Technology* (Tampere: Otatieto, 2007).

P. Weichart, "Residential Multi-Locality: In Search of Theoretical Frameworks," *Tijdschrift voor Economische en Sociale Geografie* 106: 4 (2015) 378–391.

K.S. Willis, "Situation and Connection," in A. Aurigi and F. De Cindio, ed., *Augmented Urban Spaces* (Abingdon, Oxon, GBR: Ashgate Publishing Group, 2008) 73–92.

Appendix

1. I saw that you were using your smartphone (or tablet or laptop). Would you mind telling me if you are working here?
2. How long do you usually use this space as a workplace?
3. Have you worked here before?
4. What are some of the reasons that you use this place for working?
5. What is the best feature of this space?
6. What other places have you used for working today?
7. What is the best place to work?
8. What time of the day do you use this space?
9. How many people have you been in contact with online for work-related matters while working here?
10. How many people have you been in contact with online for other matters while working here?
11. How many people have you had face-to-face contact with for work-related matters while working here?
12. With how many people have you had face-to-face contact for other matters while working here?

Contemporary Production and Urban Change: The Case of Milan

Simonetta Armondi [iD] and Antonella Bruzzese [iD]

ABSTRACT
How do new sites of production and workplaces relate to the making of urban change in Milan's peripheral areas? The paper answers this question by looking at two different fields of investigation related to peripheral areas. On one hand, the paper examines the policies promoted by the public administration at the municipal level to enhance urban innovation through new workplaces within the smart city agenda. On the other hand, the urban innovation brought by the establishment of cultural and creative industries promoted by private actors will be examined, ranging from the new geography of creative places to the creation of temporary transformations. Starting from these two fields of analysis, the paper identifies areas of difference and potential combined effects between public action and private initiative. These are placed against the backdrop of a conception of contemporary production that has worked as a tool for social inclusion and place-making in peripheral contexts in Milan.

Introduction

In this paper we reflect on new production dynamics and workspaces related to urban change, namely, new spatial practices and patterns linked with urban regeneration in the city of Milan. Using Milan as the basis of our empirical study allows us to investigate urban change by looking at the creation of new workplaces in marginal urban areas through two lenses: (1) the public policy framework aimed at enhancing the EU smart city agenda at the municipal level, and (2) the peculiar Milanese economy, which plays an important role in the establishment of cultural and creative industries.

Public policies and private initiatives that focus on economic development can construct, *via* both intentional and unintentional actions, new productive centralities—even temporary ones. Those productive centralities are located in urban areas in the case of Milan, but also fall outside the city center. Furthermore, they partially coincide with the hybrid phenomena of third-places (Oldenburg, 1989): scattered public-private hubs, fab labs, makerspaces,[1] and creative *atelier*.

The paper is organized as follows: First, the introduction covers some methodological references with an explanation of the key research questions following the literature review. Following that, the paper explains Milan's urban change from two crucial points of view: The former considers the socio-spatial dynamics and economic geography, while the latter examines the emerging spatial opportunities (periphery, shrinkage, and brownfields). The paper then focuses on the nexus of production/urban change by presenting two Milanese experiences. The first we consider to be an "unconventional" municipal urban policy approach. The second is a private driven creative production and clustering process in one particular zone of Milan, zona Tortona. We then describe lessons learned from the two different Milanese itineraries and, finally, we conclude by discussing issues that are common to all these facilities.

Regarding the research method, this is an empirical study based on document analysis and interviews. Data were collected from qualitative interviews—interviews were conducted both with individuals in charge of smart city strategies: The Councilor for Employment Policies, Economic Development, University and Research (October 2016); the Director of Economic Innovation, University, Smart City's Sector Milan Municipality (November 2015); and private actors such as promoters and entrepreneurs involved in processes of urban regeneration. These actions have been led by FabriQ's manager, the promoter of the Ventura Lambrate initiative (October 2016). The paper refers also to several interviews about the case of creative industries concentrated in Milan, conducted between 2010 and 2015, and partially used in Bruzzese (2015a) and Bruzzese and Tamini (2014) including the promoters of Zona Tortona and the Frigoriferi Milanesi regeneration project. Many documents were analyzed as well, including official documents and presentations by the city council (available on the municipality's website)[2] and others, such as National Census data, websites of newspapers, events, and workshops.[3]

Literature Review

Cities in Western countries are emerging as key places of social and economic experimentation in the twenty-first century (Glaeser, 2011; Storper, 2013; Katz and Bradley, 2013). They are changing through a shift led by three intertwined forces:

- changing work practices that include increased collaboration (Botsman and Rogers, 2010), decentralized networks, and the creation of marketplaces where the design, production, sale, and consumption of products occur
- digital technologies that have transformed traditional manufacturing as well as the management of urban services[4]
- the transition towards a knowledge- and service-based economy within contemporary capitalism (Scott, 2012).

Fab labs and makerspaces, often mixed with co-working spaces and other forms of workspace (craft and creative ateliers, manufacturing or innovation hubs), are leading to a radical reconsideration of the role of urban space in connection with complex processes of technological and organizational innovation in economic activities and in urban management. Consequently, the spatial reconfiguration of work in cities represents a key research issue in urban studies, moderately investigated in the academic debate (Gandini, 2015). Against this backdrop, there are two trajectories that we have to consider: the smart city notion and the urban creativity concept.

Re-Reading the Smart City Notion

The first focus of the paper is on place-making effects in marginal areas through smart city urban policies. The conceptualization of the "marginal area" relates to a large amount of literature on urban social exclusion in European cities (Ranci et al., 2014). We can refer to the vast debate on area-based policies that have developed over the past two decades (Power et al., 2010), or to the debate on the retrenchment of welfare state policies and austerity urbanism. However, we will emphasize the subject of the smart city. So-called "smart cities" typically fit a technical, corporatist, and neoliberal model criticized in literature (Sennett, 2012; Greenfield, 2013; Kitchin, 2014; Vanolo, 2014). Hollands (2008) for example, had already claimed a conceptualization of the "smart city" beyond the technological label. Recently, Rabari and Storper (2015) warned against the traditional narratives of the digital city as they naively stress efficiency and rational planning as a means to achieve social, economic, and environmental goals. In addition, within such a revival of old planning paradigms, these ICT narratives aim to depoliticize urban phenomena (Brenner and Schmid, 2014) and, typically, do not involve themselves in issues of social justice.

Furthermore, profound political questions regarding social inclusion, environmental sustainability, and cultural diversity go unanswered in the preconceptions about space and uniform technological solutions (McNeill, 2015). Recently, a shift in the literature aims at re-conceptualizing the smart city notion within the wider changes in urban governance, under trans-scalar political and economic pressure, related to the effects of the global financial crisis (Wiig and Wyly, 2016). Rather than celebrating or criticizing the smart city *per se*, this paper—contributing an added value to existing literature—shows the complexity of this notion and the ways it is implemented in a particular city in Southern Europe. Following Shelton et al. (2015), we point toward a nuanced, situational understanding of how and from where this "other" smart city policy model has arisen and how it is taking root in a specific place. The paper considers how and where the smart city narrative reconfigures urban governance features, but also, on the contrary, how this approach is rooted in (and shaped by) economic and social dynamics at the local scale.

Revisiting the Urban Creativity Concept

The second focus of the paper concerns pioneer projects related to creative and cultural production promoted by private actors. In Milan, several processes of urban regeneration occurred in peripheral areas and are characterized by the presence and the concentration of new production, developed by private entrepreneurs in the creative sector. The spatial concentration of creative industries in semi-central urban areas, related to production more than to consumption (Pratt, 2011), is certainly not a new phenomenon. Many scholars have analyzed the dynamics of the localization of creative activities (Lloyd, 2006), starting from the well-known cases of SoHo in New York (Zukin, 1995), the Mitte district in Berlin, and Hoxton in London (Pratt, 2009), highlighting the risks of artistic gentrification.

Concerning the clustering processes then, the spatial concentrations of cultural and creative industries can differ according to the criteria used to recognize them (Evans, 2004, 2009; Cook and Lazzaretti, 2008). Such heterogeneity reflects the variety of observed phenomena and the approaches used to face the issue. Many scholars have identified agglomerations of cultural and creative industries in recent years and named the phenomenon as "creative milieu," "cultural quarter," "creative neighborhood," or "cultural district"—putting emphasis on different aspects:

- the economic dynamics of the creative activities' clustering (Pratt, 2008) or the "district" dynamics (Becattini, 1998; Santagata, 2002; Sacco and Ferilli, 2006)
- the cultural offer and its fruition (Montgomery, 2003; Evans, 2004; McCarthy, 2005; Roodhouse, 2006)
- the "atmosphere" or urban buzz created (Storper and Venables, 2004; Storper, 2013)
- the role of the so-called creative class (Florida, 2002).

Even though there is a vast academic debate on the two contested watchwords *creativity* and *innovation*,[5] all the contributions explain, from different perspectives, the dynamics and consequences of these clustering processes of creative and cultural industries in specific areas of the city. They imply innovations in the fields of work, workplaces, and in the field of consumption and production.

Research Questions

As a result of the literature review, we have been led to the research questions that are explored in this paper:

(1) How do specific typologies of production and workspaces engender "urban change," such as new productive centralities through the reuse of vacant spaces in Milan today?
(2) How is the smart city policy understood and re-envisioned/remade through different lenses?
(3) Are privately driven processes able, and if so how, to provoke urban innovation—*via* new production—and eventually also to interact with public policies?

Milan, the icon of Italy's first "economic miracle" (Foot, 2001) during the 1950s and 1960s, is the third largest European global city (International Monetary Fund, 2015) and a noteworthy field of investigation. In fact, Milan remains, among Italian urban systems, a knowledge-economy oriented city (Mazzoleni, 2016), with a strong degree of innovation in productive activities and workplaces (Ardvisson and Colleoni, 2014; Armondi and Bolocan Goldstein, 2014; Armondi, 2015; Gandini, 2016). In particular, the city maintains a specific socioeconomic geography and spatial dynamic where urban change can stem both from the public and the private sector (Rivetti, 2013). In dealing with this issue, the paper exhibits two empirical investigations. We read together the public actions relating to a multilayered policy under the smart city urban agenda, while also considering projects from private initiatives relating to the "hybrid" creative and cultural sector.

Milan as an Empirical Study

Socio-Spatial Dynamics and Economic Geography

As noted, the socio-spatial dynamics of Milan present an original case of urban change, which relates to both a successful smart city strategy—Milan is ranked second in the

Italian smart city index (2016)—and a contemporary urban economic base. This foundation is rooted not only in traditional Milanese sectors—fashion, design, finance, and biomedical—but is now generated by new hybrid productions in the sectors of additive manufacturing, creativity, art and culture, and temporary events. Historically, Milan has been defined as the "economic capital" of Italy and its position has continued despite the dramatic global economic crisis (Magatti, 2005; Magatti and Gherardi, 2010; Magatti and Sapelli, 2012) and with the—partially unexpected—successful performance of Expo 2015. Compared to other Italian cities and urban regions, Milan's economic development is due to a combination of local and traditional economies—creativity, fashion, and technical, but also mechanical engineering, food, and ICT—along with the presence of some specialized services, such as health, higher education, research, and finance.

The Milanese entrepreneurial system has substantial features that explain its higher performance compared to the rest of the country (Camera di Commercio di Milano, 2013) including:

- the location of many larger firms and important multinational groups
- the organizational complexity, which manifests itself through the widespread presence of capital companies
- the massive tertiarization, with a solid specialization in professional services;
- a reduced manufacturing sector, but which claims productions of excellence in some leading sectors and a high capacity to create jobs
- the intensity of openness to foreign countries
- the development of some resilient forms of new entrepreneurship, such as foreign, one-person companies, which grow in general and through innovative start-ups.

Milan is also a leader in creative production. Some general data can help to depict the Milanese situation with regards to the activities included in the official census. Considering activities of the creative sector in sub-categories,[6] including "manufacturing activities," "information and communication services," "professional, scientific, and technical (architectural and engineering) activities," and "arts, sports, and entertainment activities" the active local units amount to almost 36,000, representing 19 percent of the total workforce in Milan, according to the Census of Industry and Services of 2011. The concentration of these activities in Milan is even more relevant in terms of employees, with nearly 128,000 people working in the creative production field. In absolute terms, the number of employees is less than in Rome (152,754 units), but the percentage out of the total number of employees is similar: in Milan it is 16.5 percent, in Rome 16 percent, while the national average is 9.8 percent. Creative production in Milan plays a notable role in the economic sector, but also in some urban regeneration processes, confirming dynamics that scholars have observed in recent years (Scott, 2000).

Spatial Opportunities: Periphery, Shrinkage, and Brownfields

Besides the situation briefly depicted above, we can also recognize a growing socioeconomic polarization between rich and poor—with specific spatial patterns—in Milanese urban regions that is similar to other European cities. Such polarization (Ranci, 2009) is particularly evident in some peripheral areas, particularly in neighborhoods with a strong presence of public housing that is often characterized by the presence of high levels of social vulnerability, economic vulnerability, and social disadvantage (Magatti, 2012). Some of these areas have seen several previously developed policies designed to cope with the complexity of these problems (Contratti di Quartiere, among others). Yet in recent years, they have also been the target of specific public policies aimed at supporting social inclusion, comprising the development of new jobs. In many cases, an important leverage to start these policies has been the availability of underused and abandoned spaces, often including public property.

The ground floors of many buildings owned by the public administration, in particular in public neighborhoods, contain a large number of abandoned spaces that have lost their original functions. They were for the most part shops, but also artisanal spaces or even collective and recreational spaces. They represent today an important resource as they are located in the neighborhoods of the so-called—in the Italian academic debate —"public city" (Infussi, 2011), scattered between many problematic areas. These kinds of units: shops, workshops, warehouses, and offices (i.e., different from residences), located in buildings owned by the municipality of Milan, today number 869. Their average surface area is about 60 square meters and the neighborhoods with the highest number of these types of spaces can be found in Quarto Oggiaro, Chiesa Rossa, and Niguarda.[7]

The abandonment of areas and buildings in Milan and in other western cities concerns several typologies of spaces presenting different sizes and localizations as the literature on shrinkage has shown (Oswalt and Rieniets, 2006; Armondi, 2011; Martinez-Fernandez et al., 2012). Consequently, there are varying impacts on the neighboring areas as well as complex problems and opportunities for the city (Armondi, 2013; Lanzani et al., 2014; Lanzani, 2015). In Milan, a significant number of the abandoned spaces concern former industrial areas. The industrial past of the city has been marked both by big companies—such as Pirelli, Breda, Innocenti, Maserati, and Ansaldo that were historically based in large plants located in peripheral urban areas —and dozens of productive firms of medium size in neighborhoods just outside the city center. The urban economy's profound restructuring process that transformed Milan from an industrial city into a center of tertiary advanced services (Camera di Commercio, 2015), and the related abandonment processes, started in the 1980s with both the closure and relocation of industry. These changes left an availability of more than five million square meters of former industrial abandoned areas, representing approximately 4 percent of the urbanized area (Lombardy Region's Geoportale, 2014). Ninety percent of this area's surface is composed of large lots,[8] many of which are vacant, due to the current stagnating real estate market conditions and their size.[9] The other 10 percent (equal to 80 percent of the lots) are lots of less than 20,000 square meters. In comparison to the larger ones, they are often located in the compact urban fabric of Milan in functionally mixed areas where residences are integrated with production and trade. Consequently, they represent a significant spatial opportunity that has allowed several private renewal interventions, such as creative industries, but also fab labs, makerspaces, and co-working facilities that traditionally reuse existing spaces.

Two Trajectories on the Nexus of New Productions/Urban Change in Milan

A New Smart Urban Policy between the Social and the Spatial

As described, Milan remains, among the Italian urban systems, a knowledge-based economy city, with a strong degree of innovation in production activities and new workplaces. Nevertheless, Milan displays a contradictory urban transformation, including a pervasive process of spatial shrinkage, social exclusion, marginalization, and conflict, along with an utter desolation in the midst of the areas of greatest abundance (Andreotti, 2006). The city appears more as a place of contradiction and a site of contest, rather than a coherent whole. Paradoxically, the Municipality of Milan has assumed this latter condition as a strength, rather than a weakness, using it to build a new style of public policy. In Milan, the emergence of a more pluralistic frame of urban governance, since the election of the previous Mayor Giuliano Pisapia, has contributed to the redefinition of the roles played by the local authority and economic and social actors.

On the one hand, Milan displays a large, triumphalist approach to urban transformation projects, such as with the mobilization of Expo 2015. On the other hand, Milan is changing through a much more spatially diffused and minimal way. The micro and spatially spread processes of economic and social initiatives are shaping new productive centralities in the city. In particular, Milan's recent left-wing local leadership has made investments beyond just large-scale development projects.[10] Rather, the municipality has tried to reinforce a more inclusive and shared approach by letting the local authority act simultaneously as an enabler and partner.

The City of Milan, beginning in June 2011 with the City Council led by Mayor Giuliano Pisapia, and continuing with the new mayor Giuseppe Sala in June 2016—whose election campaign was marked by the motto "urban periphery is my main obsession"—has chosen to promote social innovation as one of the aspects of the smart city framework (Comune di Milano, 2014). Thus in 2012, the municipality developed a strategy for its smart city agenda based on coordination rather than implementation (Gascó et al., 2015). Responsibility for the coordination effort was given to the Councilor for Employment Policies, Economic Development, University and Research, a member of the municipal government, as well as to a municipal manager, the head of the department in charge of Economic Innovation, Smart City, and University.

The underlying vision of the Milanese public policy approach is, therefore, one in which a smart city not only cultivates its technological component, but recognizes, according to the recent debate (Gill Garcia et al., 2015), that a smart city concept can be a multifaceted and place-based concept. The unusual Milanese approach to smartness is "between the social and the spatial" (De Boiser et al., 2016), as it is based on the use of new technologies, while also combining economic development with social inclusion, infrastructures and human capital, innovation and training, and research and participation. Therefore, it inspires smart policies focused not only on the potentials of ICTs but also on vulnerable population targets (older people, children, young people, people with disabilities, migrants), in order to increase equal opportunities and deal with discrimination. At the same time, the municipality explores all the policy tools necessary to provide the framework and internal coordination, by bringing together different players, along with public and private resources.

In general, social innovation, as a principle, can be assumed to be the antithesis of conventional smart city rhetoric (Moulaert et al., 2013). The attempt of the Milanese Municipality to create an unprecedented framework based on a mix of private and public investment is to join these two different discourses and practices. Two dates are crucial to understanding how the Councilor for Employment Policies, Economic Development, University, and Research with the Councilor of Metropolitan Area, Housing, and Public Property has reshaped traditional styles of policy in their field. The organizing committee of Milan Smart City—based on a key alliance between the Municipality and Chamber of Commerce—organized a public event on April 19, 2013 at the National Museum of Science and Technology, entitled "Public Hearing: Smart City towards Milano Smart City." This was the first national forum on smart cities with the goal of involving the main stakeholders of the city in creating a system of consultation and a governance network. On July 18, 2013, a second day of debate was held, entitled "Open Innovation: Social Ideas and Strategies for Milano Smart City," where questions were raised about how the municipality could intervene to favor enterprises that deal with social innovation.

The result is the delineation of the so-called "Milan IN-policy" frame, based on the following interrelated dimensions:

- innovation on a strategic level to foster development and competitiveness of the local/regional economic system, including policy making and financial resources that Milan invests in innovative starts ups, fab labs, incubators, and the sharing economy
- social innovation/inclusion, through employment inclusion and digital inclusion, thanks to the collaborative economy and initiatives in critical neighborhoods.

The new policy approach is also joined with the Municipality resolution n. 1978/2012. This resolution focuses on the reuse of vacant public real estate, introducing a new urban policy to foster economic development and social inclusion

As a first act, the Municipality promoted several public actions aimed at occupying vacant public properties, including the construction of Co-Hub, a new micro-district in the historic center of Milan in Vicolo Calusca. This hub opened in November 2015 and introduced citizens and entrepreneurs to the sharing economy, the ongoing Smart City Lab in Via Ripamonti 88, and the ongoing renewal of a vacant old industrial building, Mhuma (Milano Hub Makers) as a new incubator for makers and digital manufacturing. Mhuma is owned by the municipality in Via d'Azeglio, between Brera and Corso Como, in the historical city center. Furthermore, this first dimension is related to the ongoing new innovative mixed-use space, Base, located in the heart of Zona Tortona, with the regeneration of a vacant industrial building (over 6,000 square meters of the former Ansaldo steelworks) that has always been owned by the municipality.

Against the backdrop of new co-sharing workplaces and new centers of production, in addition to the register of accredited co-working spaces—currently 58 with a total of 364 coworkers (Camera di Commercio di Milano, 2013)—the municipality and the Milan Chamber of Commerce have launched the call "Creative Makers" (Comune di Milano, 2013). This call has established nine accredited FabLabs on redeveloped vacant public properties. The second dimension establishes ad hoc public actions focused on the nexus between workplaces and social innovation, located in what the municipality defines as "peripheral neighborhoods." Two initiatives are crucial: the FrabiQ incubator and the call for proposals, "Tira su la Cler." FabriQ, in the Quarto Oggiaro neighborhood, is an incubator for social economy and innovation, which started in January 2014. Quarto Oggiaro is a deprived and marginal public housing neighborhood built in the 1960s for immigrants from southern Italy. Today it suffers from social segregation, poverty, diffused micro criminality, and an overall high rate of unemployment (youth unemployment is around 70 percent). FabriQ is open to social enterprises, but also to for-profit enterprises with a clear social attitude. The incubator offers services designed to support financial, organizational, and logistical difficulties, which are often encountered during the setting up of business activities, particularly in the social sector. The selected companies have access to financial aid, nine months of incubation, tutoring programs, co-working facilities, and instructional workshops.

In December 2014, FabriQ launched a call for proposals with a budget of €146,000. The call had two distinctive features: the possibility of participation for foreign enterprises and the definition of the three project themes of "smart city," sharing economy, and accessibility. After the very successful first call, FabriQ launched another call in October 2016 (FabriQ, 2016). Through the call "Tira su la Cler" (2014), built with the involvement of the Neighborhood Councils (Consigli di Zona), the Councilor of Employment Policies and Economic Development allocated €206,630 for microenterprises including artisans, independent entrepreneurs, and cooperatives who intend to open a new business in the neighborhood. Over 50 percent of the proposals were presented by young entrepreneurs. The Councilor of the Public Property has identified and made available to companies a range of vacant properties on the ground floor of public residential buildings in three critical neighborhoods: Quarto Oggiaro, Chiesa Rossa, and Niguarda. Four units are small (under 50 square meters), two are medium sized (50–75 square meters), and three are larger (75–120 square meters). The new activities include: a video production enterprise, a workshop for furnishing and interior restoration, a shop dedicated to sports clothing, an activity for parks design and gardening with a space dedicated to the dissemination of green culture, a store dedicated to sustainable mobility with bicycles, skateboards, electric bikes and everything that helps the dissemination of a no-oil culture. The business projects have rent reductions of up to 90 percent for the first five years, in addition to financial resources for both interior renewal and startup project strengthening.

Creative Productions and Clustering Processes via Private Actions

As stated above, the creative and cultural industries in Milan are deeply relevant to the urban economy, especially with the increasing specialization in advanced services in the last decades (Bolocan and Bonfantini, 2007). Milan is known both as a capital of fashion—represented mostly by the big brand shops in the so called "fashion quadrilateral" around via Montenapoleone in the city center (Janson and Power, 2010; d'Ovidio, 2008)—and as a capital of design. In Milan, the establishment of creative activities is a "long-term" story (D'Ovidio, 2015; D'Ovidio, Pradel, 2013), which occurred thanks to the synergy of the manufacturing system of the Lombardy region (Branzi, 2003), and the education and training networks linked with the universities (Balducci et al., 2010).

Creative productions have had a driving role not only in the urban economy, but also in regeneration processes of semi-central areas in the city in recent years, especially through processes of "concentrations" of similar activities. Despite the several definitions of clustering processes of creative industries, as briefly listed above, in the case of Milan we refer to them as "creative urban concentrations" (Bruzzese, 2015a, 2015b). We identify the presence of a relevant number of creative activities—e.g., design, architecture, graphic design, publishing, exhibition spaces, laboratories, design studios, photographic studios, spaces for rehearsals, etc.—and also of peculiar qualitative elements, such as:

- the high reputation of some creative activities (able more than others to mobilize interests, both at the local and supra-local scale)
- the overlapping of activities' localization and temporary events related to *Fuorisalone* (see below), which over the years has created a sort of ephemeral geography in Milano
- the use of promotional and place-branding interventions of various kinds, aimed at improving the reputation of the areas, hosting creative industries and creative events (Bruzzese et al., 2013)
- the public status that in recent years put these areas on the map as the creative places in Milan.

In particular, the districts known as *Zona Tortona* (Knox, 2015) and *Ventura Lambrate* (Bruzzese, 2015c) represent significant cases of Milanese "creative concentration." They also serve as examples of how certain types of "work" have been able to start reuse processes and to reactivate new economies, new practices, and new images of the city, replacing the industrial past with a new professionalism related to the knowledge economy (OECD, 1997; Rullani, 2008; Scott, 2012; Powell and Snellman, 2004).

The areas affected by these phenomena have the followings recurring characteristics:

- They are located in semi-central positions at the edge of the city center, yet close to railroads and some infrastructural nodes. Those features provide a high level of accessibility.
- They have a strong presence of medium-sized manufacturing firms. This condition provides flexibility to meet the needs of creative industries. Moreover, there is the possibility to be transformed at relatively affordable costs by private operators within a relatively simple normative framework.[11]
- These areas are affected by mixed uses, presenting a number of spaces still available to be transformed.

All these conditions have been permitted in the last 15 to 20 years through an incremental process of urban transformation, in which the "pioneer interventions" have been followed by other similar interventions in the available buildings with similar characteristics located in the surroundings. Their protagonists have often been entrepreneurs that overlapped with the creative class. In fact, many of these "pioneer projects" have been promoted by fashion and design operators themselves, as in the case of *Superstudio più* in Zona Tortona, one of the most established cases among the Milanese creative concentrations. The district is located beyond the Milanese railway belt, but still well connected to public transportation. In the past it was characterized by the presence of old factories and former workers' residences.[12] It has now become, in the urban (and global) imagination, one of the "creative quarters," the location of many creative industries and the center of the Fuorisalone events, as we will see later.

Here, during the 1980s, the pioneer intervention was made by the photographers and fashion operators who transformed a former industrial building into the "Superstudio," a space for photo shoots, exhibitions, and art publishing. Superstudio—thanks to its success and the appeal of its managers— began an incremental process in the area around via Tortona that produced, between 1985 and 2015, the transformation of 14 industrial buildings from traditional manufacturing to creative activities by private entrepreneurs[13] (Bruzzese, 2015a; Giuliani, 2015). The public administration has been absent until the last few years until, in the former Ansaldo industrial precinct complex, MUDEC and Base began operations, becoming the only public interventions in the area. MUDEC is the Museum of Cultures and Base the "hybrid center for culture and creativity, whose main objective is to renovate the relation between culture and economy, between democracy, well-being, the knowledge economy, social innovation, and development," assigned *via* public bid by a group of social entrepreneurs.[14]

In the Tortona area, the regeneration of abandoned industrial areas in most cases did not lead to demolition and replacement, but rather to the refurbishment of the original plants. The establishment of creative and experimental activities in Tortona was deeply intertwined with the presence of recursive temporary events and initiatives, such as Fashion Week and especially the *Fuorisalone*.[15] This matching between temporary events and the regeneration of places is the peculiarity of the case of Milan. These transitory events, in fact, have not only been able to temporarily "turn on" some spaces and attract a large number of people, but have also made neglected urban areas more known and recognizable. This has helped to increase awareness of their potentialities, stimulating the interest of several private operators interested in promoting locally-based "creative *zones.*" Such branding activity has fostered—together with the other factors mentioned above (i.e. flexibility, accessibility, availability of spaces)—the setting up and launch of further transitory and permanent creative activities in these areas. Indirectly, they also activated a sort of social innovation. Several local associations in fact, especially in the Ventura Lambrate area, have been influenced by these initiatives and have promoted a different kind of activism looking for synergies with the effects brought by creative production. These activities include the organization of ethical fashion shows, or actions to prolong the positive effects of temporary design week.[16]

A wide literature about gentrification (Glass, 1964; Zukin, 1982; Atkinson and Bridge, 2005; Semi, 2015) expresses severe criticism of creative concentrations as a main gentrifying process and the "invasion" of new users accessing global and extraordinary dynamics to stifle local and daily ones. Nonetheless, it is worth noting the opinions of local resident associations in Milan. They reveal the desire to permanently activate the "dynamism" developed by the presence of creative production and temporary cultural events to overcome its intermittent condition (currently activity only occurs in specific periods of the year). Moreover, they want to exploit the events themselves, as a means to improve the quality of urban life as a whole, by bridging the gap between local residents and "creative" or temporary users. Several local associations[17] are trying to establish a dialogue with the world of creativity and the dynamics of the *Fuorisalone* to build partnerships for the service of the territory. They are attempts to engender this synergy within the exogenous logic of the creative events. The successful processes of urban regeneration in the Tortona and Ventura Lambrate areas, promoted by entrepreneurs, has inspired not only new networks of entrepreneurs, but also local actors and local associations working in the neighborhood interested in social innovation.

Lessons from Milan's Urban Change

The urban change reported in this paper sheds light on two different shifts: one initiated by public institutions through an unconventional policy style, and another involving private actors, particularly in the creative sector. The paper has recognized that the potentialities of Milan's urban change depends on specific hidden and disclosed resources of a very high number of diverse, micro and macro, private, collective, and public actors. The paper has offered an analysis of the production/urban change nexus *via* both public actions and individual private actions focusing on three research questions.

First, we have shown that the smart city agenda can have a subtle impact on urban change and on social inclusion through the support of new productions. We have argued for a focus on smart city urban policy as it "actually exists" (Shelton et al., 2015).

- We have shown a completely innovative approach to smart city policy. In fact, the "Milan model" of smart city policy has the potential to contest the existing neoliberal smart city framings criticized in literature. The paper has underlined the way in which smart city policy was instituted, the style and the method through which new workspaces and enterprises were realized, and the way in which public actions were implemented. These have occurred by joining several urban issues: e.g., vacant public properties in peripheral areas and the need for new entrepreneurship, or the implementation of innovative horizontal networks inside the municipality—between councilors—and outside with private actors.[18] In particular, the involvement of the Chamber of Commerce reflects, contrary to some urban policy (Evans, 2009), the trust in traditional enterprise agencies.
- The municipality seems aware, according to Rittel and Webber (1973) and Harrison (2000), that urban policy deals with "wicked problems." Consequently, the public actor assumes that the wicked problems in Milan, are "essentially unique" (Rittel and Webber, 1973). Consequently, for each of them, the councilors and their staff have built an ad hoc project. In Milan, we recognize an urban policy mobility (Robinson, 2015), where rather than tracing policies until they arrive somewhere, a variegated spatiality of policy mobility emerges when considering how policies are "arrived at." In particular, in this incremental framework, the smart city notion adapts to and matches the variety of spatial conditions and socioeconomic dynamics. It is not merely a sector of urban policy.
- Consequent complexities and uncertainties, as well as the tendency towards a more localized welfare provision (Andreotti and Mingione, 2016) affected by the economic crisis, challenges a traditional approach of the ex-ante centralized program where clearly standard objectives and actions consistent with each other define timelines and distribute investments. Rather, the local administration takes a design approach that Charles Lindblom (1959) has called "muddling through," which takes on the "urban" opportunities that occur step by step.

Second, private-led creative production initiatives in Milan have been an interesting engine of urban change for several reasons:

- They have filled many urban voids with new production activities. The availability of an abandoned urban fabric, with medium-size buildings that private operators have renovated autonomously, has been a real spatial asset that has influenced the localization of the regeneration processes of the former industrial areas.
- They have been able to intervene on a symbolic level, promoting new urban images that in some cases have been successful and triggered other movements of inhabitants to revive other neighborhood images (in some cases the initiatives of several local associations have been synergic with those of other more market-oriented actors). This is also due to the nature of these places, between places of production and places of consumption with a "hybrid" nature, which can be an interesting novelty affecting different areas and create new forms of jobs.
- The effects of gentrification are not very relevant in the case of Ventura Lambrate where there is a balance between new productions, "old" inhabitants, and new users. In Tortona, however, the effects are more present.[19] In Ventura Lambrate there has been—up until now—a mutual influence between creative production, urban regeneration, and social innovation, shown clearly in the increased liveliness of the associations' initiatives.
- These kinds of process have been privately driven with public actors absent. Nonetheless, since the election of Mayor Giuliano Pisapia, the local administration has recognized their relevance, not only towards improving the urban economy, but also towards mobilizing social innovation in peripheral areas. The recent initiative promoted by the city of Milan during Fall Design Week 2016 worked exactly towards enhancing synergies between public and private actors.

Conclusions

This paper is pioneering in its attempts to understand the process of urban change through an integrated analysis of the initiatives of private actors and institutional perspectives. Furthermore, the findings make a novel contribution to research describing the development of a smart city framework in a specific urban context marked by a climate of minor, but multiple creative and cultural practices. As a consequence, in Milan, urban change is not only the intentional effect of institutional strategies and smart city public policies. Rather, it is the—sometimes unintended—outcome of the mobilization of a complex and pluralistic network of local and non-local actors.

After years characterized by a top-down relationship between government and citizens, the left-wing government, using smart city as a policy tool, began working to include stakeholders, citizens, start-uppers, and entrepreneurs. This new decision-making and planning process relates to: first, a spatial focus on the vacant spaces of peripheral areas; second, a new production paradigm, broadly considered. Another important feature of the new administration phase is the promotion of temporary events, activities, and spatial regeneration initiatives. They are able to involve external visitors but also the citizens of Milan.

To conclude, Milan's change in its overall urban trajectory emerges from a peculiar intersection of several diverse actions and investment arrangements. The role of local government in the public/private relationship has been emphasized by the Councilor for Employment Policies, Economic Development, University, and Research, as "on one hand, to promote networking of weak manifold practices of private local actors; on the other hand, to define framing activities related to the multiplicity of urban initiatives." (Interview, December 2016). In fact, as shown in this paper, in recent years, the local government and a complex network of nonprofit, quasi-public, and private actors have been able to frame a shared vision, shifting the public policy approach from a traditional smart city notion and pro-growth development model towards an unconventional type of public policy. This vision is founded on the mobilization of the local civil society, the valorization and attraction of talent, and the support given to—along with the active involvement of—new productions, workplaces, and entrepreneurial initiatives. These experiences are at an early stage, but they make evident that inclusive socioeconomic development patterns are possible.

Notes

1. A fab lab (fabrication laboratory) is a small-scale workshop offering (personal) digital fabrication. A makerspace is a community center that provides technology, manufacturing equipment, and educational opportunities to the public (see Moriset, 2014 and Mariotti et al. in this issue).
2. See all the documents available at: www.lavoroeformazioneincomune.it
3. During the workshop "I luoghi della produzione creativa a Milano. Riflessioni e prospettive" ("The Places of Creative Production in Milan: Reflections and Perspectives"), held at the Triennale di Milan, May 22, 2013, the curators—A. Bruzzese, I. Giuliani, C. Botti—collected the views both of four scholars working on the issue and four entrepreneurs involved in the process.
4. See the *Journal of Urban Technology* special issue: "Creating Smart-er Cities" 18:2 (2011).
5. For critical interpretation of the notion of creative class and creative city respectively, see Peck 2005 and Scott 2006. On the link between the city and innovation, see Shearmur 2012.
6. The list of the sub-categories used is visible in Bruzzese 2015b. How to define, and consequently quantify, creative production sectors is an open question. To understand the Italian situation, see Fondazione Symbola's 2015 report.
7. Data from Cognetti 2014.
8. The surfaces vary between 20,000 and 600,000 square meters, and the number of lots equals to the 20 percent of the total number.
9. For an interesting and still actual portrait of the "unfinished" Milan see Bolocan Goldstein and Bonfantini 2007.
10. For a synthesis of Milan's previous urban policy see Gonzaléz 2009.
11. This framework has allowed operators to begin their works with a direct intervention method called DIA (Dichiarazione di Inizio Attività). Nowadays, for buildings larger than 15,000 square meters, this would imply the use of an implementation plan (Piano Attuativo), accompanied by a transfer of standards areas and a share of at least 35 percent of social housing.
12. The area is about 1 square kilometer with 15,175 residents. 7.4 percent of the buildings are productive (the Milanese average is 5.8 percent), 8.1 percent tertiary and offices (the Milanese average is 4.4 percent) See Milan's PGT (general urban plan), adopted in 2012. Annex 3, Le 88 Schede NIL.
13. Including some big fashion brands such as Esprit, Kenzo, Zegna, Hugo Boss, Gas, Diesel, Tod's and the Armani museum.

14. More information on www.base.milano.it
15. *Fuorisalone* is the set of initiatives, events, trade fairs and creative activities that happen in the city, while Milan's annual International Furniture Fair (Salone del Mobile) takes place at the fairgrounds. At the beginning of the 1980s, this was a spontaneous phenomenon involving only young and emerging designers, seeking alternative locations around the city. Year after year this trend gradually expands, giving birth in the 1990s to the "*Fuorisalone*" as it is nowadays: a big number of events, that takes place in industrial spaces, streets, showroom, and galleries in several districts of Milan, attracted more than 350,000 visitors in 2014.
16. The motto of the local association Made in Lambrate is: "the neighborhood that is alive 365 days a year."
17. Such as Made in Lambrate, or Association Tortona, or Cascina Cuccagna to name a few.
18. The Councilor for Employment Policies, Economic Development, University and Research underlines that "In the last five years, thanks to new smart city policies, 63 spaces for new production available for citizens were created, and 40.000 square meters of vacant spaces were renewed" (Tajani, 2016).
19. In these areas a certain heterogeneity still exists, both in the inhabitant's social profiles and in the economic activities' profiles. The place where the effects of gentrification are more visible is in the Tortona area. Here the real estate average price in the period from 1993 to 2012 increased considerably. For example, for "new apartments" prices jumped from 2.450 €/sq.m to approximately 5.050 €/sq.m (+205 percent); for "recent apartments (with less than 40 years and refurbished)" from 1.800 to 4.000 (+221 percent); and "apartments, with more than 40 years or to refurbish" from 1.420 to 3.150 (+222 percent) (OSMI, 2012). Although it appears high, the increase is in line with the trend of Milanese prices during the same period and it is not so different from others registered in neighboring areas (for example, the homologous data in the nearby area "Conca del Naviglio," which are + 180 percent; + 190 percent; + 164 percent respectively).

Disclosure statement

No potential conflict of interest was reported by the authors.

ORCID

Simonetta Armondi http://orcid.org/0000-0001-5293-7581
Antonella Bruzzese http://orcid.org/0000-0001-9785-7606

Bibliography

A. Arvidsson, and E. Colleoni, "Knowledge sharing and social capital building. The role of co-working spaces in the knowledge economy in Milan", (Unpublished Report, Office for Youth, Municipality of Milan, 2014).

S. Armondi, *Disabitare. Storie di spazi separati* (Sant'Arcangelo di Romagna: Maggioli, 2011).

S. Armondi, "What We Talk About When We Talk About Productive Territories. The Case of Shrinking Italy," *The International Journal of Architectonic, Spatial, and Environmental Design*, 6: 3 (2013) 61–76.

S. Armondi, and M. Bolocan Goldstein, "Urban Space and Geography of Production in the 21st Century: Notes from Milan" Paper Presented at the *EURA - European Urban Research Association Conference* (Paris 2014).

S. Armondi, "Spazio urbano, nuove geografie del lavoro e della produzione. Una lettura internazionale," *Imprese & Città* 8 (2015) 30–42.

A. Andreotti, "Milan: Urban Poverty in a Wealthy City" in S. Musterd, A. Murie. eds. *Neighborhoods of Poverty: Urban Social Exclusion and Integration in Comparison Europe* (London: Palgrave Macmillan 2006) 87–112.

A. Andreotti, and E. Mingione, "Local Welfare Systems in Europe and the Economic Crisis," *European Urban and Regional Studies* 23:3 (2016) 252–266.

R. Atkinson, and G. Bridge, eds., *Gentrification in A Global Contest. The New Urban Colonialism* (New York, London: Routledge, 2005).

A. Balducci, F. Cognetti and V. Fedeli, eds., *Milano, la città degli studi. Storia, geografia e politiche delle università milanesi* (Milano: Abitare Segesta Cataloghi Collana AIM, 2010).

G. Becattini, *Distretti Industriali e Made in Italy* (Torino: Bollati Boringhieri, 1998).

M. Bolocan Goldstein, and B. Bonfantini, *Milano incompiuta. Interpretazioni urbanistiche del mutamento* (Milano: Franco Angeli, 2007).

R. Botsman, and R. Rogers, *What's Mine Is Yours: The Rise of Collaborative Consumption* (USA: Harper Collins, 2010).

A. Branzi, "Milano Distretto per L'innovazione," *Impresa & Stato* 62: (2003) 35–42.

N. Brenner, and C. Schmid, "The 'Urban Age' in Question," *International Journal of Urban and Regional Research* 38: 3 (2014) 731–755.

A. Bruzzese, *Addensamenti Creativi, Trasformazioni Urbane e Fuorisalone* (Santarcangelo di Romagna: Maggioli, 2015a).

A. Bruzzese, "The Places of Creative Production. Concentrations, Features and Urban Transformation Processes in Milan" Paper Presented at the Annual Meeting on Cultural Heritage 4th Conference, *Cultural Creative Industries: economic development and urban regeneration*, (Rome 2015b).

A. Bruzzese, "Spazi in Attesa, Industria Creativa e Riusi Temporanei. Il Caso Di Lambrate a Milano" Paper Presented at the Conferenza Nazionale SIU, (Venezia 2015c).

A. Bruzzese, and L. Tamini, *Servizi Commerciali e Produzioni creative. Sei itinerari nella Milano che cambia* (Milano: Bruno Mondadori, 2014).

A. Bruzzese, C. Botti, and I. Giuliani, "Territorial Branding Strategies Behind and Beyond Visions of Urbanity. The Role of the Fuorisalone Event in Milan," *Planum. The Journal of Urbanism* 28: 2 (2013) 44–51.

Camera di Commercio, *Milano Produttiva, Annual Report 2015* (Milano: Bruno Mondadori, 2015).

Camera di Commercio di Milano, Avviso pubblico per Costituzione di un elenco qualificato di soggetti fornitori di servizi di coworking nella città di Milano. Erogazione di incentivi economici a favore di giovani coworkers, 2013 available at http://www.mi.camcom.it/c/document_library/get_file?uuid=01c2ece9-587e-4a96-a445-006d65e10a2c&groupId=10157 (accessed October 2016).

Comune di Milano, Bando Creative Makers 2013, available at https://www.comune.milano.it/dseserver/webcity/garecontratti.nsf/51607b595b240841c1256c4500569c90/8d3b6a258e2d2804c1257b980040c31e/$FILE/Bando%20CREATIVE%20MAKERS.pdf. (accessed October 2016).

F. Cognetti, ed., *Vuoti A Rendere* (Milano: Fondazione Politecnico di Milano, 2014).

P. Cook, and L. Lazzaretti, eds., *Creative Cities, Cultural Clusters and Local Economic Development* (Northampton: Edward Elgar Publishing, 2008).

Comune di Milano, Guidelines Milano Smart City (Milano: Comune di Milano, May 2014). http://www.milanosmartcity.org/. Accessed October 15, 2016.

K. De Boyser, C. Dewilde, D. Dierckx, and J. Friedrichs, eds, *Between the Social and the Spatial* (New York, London: Routledge, 2016).

M. D'Ovidio, "The Field of Fashion Production in Milan: A Theoretical Discussion and an Empirical Investigation," *City, Culture and Society* 2: 6 (2015) 1–8.

M. D'Ovidio, and M. Pradel, "Social Innovation and Institutionalization in the Cognitive-Cultural Economy: two Contrasting Experiences From Southern Europe," *Cities* 33: (2013) 69–76.

M. D'Ovidio, "Tessuti Sociali. Relazioni, Spazio, Creatività Nell'industria Della Moda a Milano", *AIS Giovani Sociologi*, (Napoli: ScriptaWeb, 2008) 147–166.

G. Evans, "Cultural Industry Quarters: From Pre-Industrial to Post-Industrial Production", in Bell D., Jayne M., eds., *City of Quarters: Urban Villages in the Contemporary City*, (Aldershot: Ashgate, 2004) 71–92.

G. Evans, "From Cultural Quarters to Creative Cluster – Creative Spaces in the New City Economy", in M. Legnér, D. Ponzini, eds., *Cultural Quarters and Urban Transformation: International Perspectives*, (Klintehamn: Gotlandica förlag, 2009) 34–61.

R.L. Florida, *The Rise of the Creative Class: and how It's Transforming Work, Leisure, Community and Everyday Life* (New York, NY: Basic Books 2002).

FabriQ, Call for Social Innovators 2016, available at http://www.fabriq.eu/call-4-social-innovators/ (accessed October 2016).

Fondazione Symbola – Unioncamere, *Io sono cultura*, (Report 2015).

M. Foot, *Milan Since the Miracle: City, Culture and Identity* (Oxford: Berg, 2001).

A. Gandini, "The Rise of Coworking Space: A Literature Review," *Ephemera Journal* 15: 1 (2015) 193–205.

A. Gandini, *The Reputation Economy: Understanding Knowledge Work in Digital Society* (London: Palgrave Macmillan, 2016).

M. Gascó, B. Trivellato, and D. Cavenago, "How Do Southern European Cities Foster Innovation? Lessons from the Experience of the Smart City Approaches of Barcelona and Milan" in J.R. Gill Garcia, T.A. Pardo, T. Nam, eds., *Smarter as the New Urban Agenda: A Comprehensive View of the 21st Century City*, (Switzerland: Springer, 2015) 191–206.

E.L., Glaeser, *Triumph of the City: How Our Greatest Invention Makes Us Richer, Smarter, Greener, Healthier, and Happier* (London: Penguin Press, 2011).

J.R. Gill Garcia, T.A. Pardo, and T. Nam, eds., *Smarter as the New Urban Agenda: A Comprehensive View of the 21st Century City* (Switzerland: Springer, 2015).

R. Glass, "Introduction: Aspects of Change" in Centre for Urban Studies (ed.), *London: aspects of change*, MacGibbon and Kee XIII, XLII London (1964).

S. González, "(Dis)Connecting Milan(ese): Deterritorialised Urbanism and Disempowering Politics in Globalizing Cities," *Environment and Planning A* 41: (2009) 31–47.

A. Greenfield, *Against the Smart City* (New York: Do Projects, 2013).

T. Harrison, "Urban Policy: Addressing Wicked Problems" in S. Nutley, P. Smith, H. Davis, eds. *What Works? Evidence-Based Policy and Practice in Public Services* (Bristol: Policy Press, 2000) 13–41.

R.G. Hollands, "Will the Real Smart City Please Stand up?" *City: Analysis of Urban Trends, Culture, Theory, Policy, Action* 12: 3 (2008) 303–320.

F. Infussi, ed., *Dal recinto al territorio. Milano, esplorazioni nella città pubblica* (Milano: Bruno Mondadori, 2011).

International Monetary Fund, *World Economic Outlook*, Report (2015 April).

Italian Smart City Index, Report Ernst & Young (2016).

B. Katz, and J. Bradley, *The Metropolitan Revolution: How Cities and Metros Are Fixing Our Broken Politics and Fragile Economy* (Washington: The Brookings Institution, 2013).

R. Kitchin, "The Real-Time City? Big Data and Smart Urbanism," *GeoJournal* 79: 1 (2014) 1–14.

P. Knox, ed., *Atlante Delle Città* (Milano: Hoepli, 2015).

A. Lanzani, *Città, territorio, urbanistica tra crisi e contrazione* (Milano: Franco Angeli, 2015).

A. Lanzani, C. Merlini, and F. Zanfi, "Quando "un nuovo ciclo di vita" non si dà. Fenomenologia dello spazio abbandonato e prospettive per il progetto urbanistico oltre il paradigma del riuso," *Archivio di Studi Urbani e Regionali* 109: (2014) 28–47.

Ch. E. Lindblom, "The Science of Muddling Through," *Public Administration Review* 19: 2 (1959) 79–88.

R.D. Lloyd, *Neo-Bohemia: Art and Commerce in the Postindustrial City* (New York, NY, London: Routledge, 2006).

J. Jansson, D. Power, "Fashioning A Global City: Global City Brand Channels in the Fashion and Design Industries," *Regional Studies* 44: 44 (2010) 889–904.

M. Magatti, et al. eds., *Milano, Nodo Della Rete Globale. Un Itinerario Di Analisi e Proposte* (Milano: Bruno Mondadori, 2005).

M. Magatti, L. Gherardi, eds., *The City of Flows. Territories, Agencies and Institutions* (Milano: Bruno Mondadori, 2010).

M. Magatti, *La Città Abbandonata. Dove Sono e Come Cambiano Le Periferie Italiane* (Bologna: Il Mulino, 2012).

M. Magatti, and G. Sapelli, eds., *Progetto Milano. Idee e Proposte Per La Città Di Domani* (Milano: Bruno Mondadori, 2012).

C. Martinez-Fernandez, I. Audirac, S. Fol, and E. Cunningham-Sabot, "Shrinking Cities: Urban Challenges of Globalization," *International Journal of Urban and Regional Research*, 36:2, (2012) 213–225.

I. Mariotti, C. Pacchi, S. Di Vita, "Coworking Spaces in Milan: ICTs, Proximity, and Urban Effects," *Journal of Urban Technology*, 2017 forthcoming.

C. Mazzoleni, "Knowledge-Creating Activities in Contemporary Metropolitan Areas, Spatial Rationales and Urban Policies: Evidence from the Case Study of Milan", in A. Cusinato, A. Philippopoulos-Mihalopoulos, eds. *Knowledge-creating Milieus in Europe*, (Berlin: Springer, 2016) 118–141.

J. McCarthy, "Making Spaces for Creativity: Designating "Cultural Quarters" (41st ISoCaRP Congress 2005).

D. McNeill, "Global Firms and Smart Technologies: IBM and the Reduction of the City," *Transactions of the Institute of British Geographers* 40: 4 (2015) 562–574.

J. Montgomery, "Cultural Quarters as Mechanisms for Urban Regeneration, Part 1: Conceptualizing Cultural Quarters," *Planning Practice and Research* 18: 4 (2003) 293–306.

B. Moriset, "Building New Places of the Creative Economy. The Rise of Coworking Spaces," Paper Presented at the 2nd Geography of Innovation International Conference (Utrecht, January 2014).

F. Moulaert, E. Swyngedouw, F. Martinelli and S. Gonzalez, eds., *Can Neighborhoods Save the City? Community Development and Social Innovation* (London: Routledge, 2010).

OECD, *The Knowledge Based Economy* (Paris, OECD /GD 102, 1997).

R. Oldenburg, *The Great Good Place* (New-York: Paragon House, 1989).

OSMI, *Borsa Immobiliare, 42° Edizione Rilevazione Prezzi Immobili Milano e Provincia* (Milano: Rapporto, 2012).

P. Oswalt and T. Rieniets, eds., *Atlas of Shrinking Cities* (Ostfildern-Ruit: Hatje Cantz Verlag, 2006).

J. Peck, "Struggling with the Creative Class" *International Journal of Urban and Regional Research*, 29: 4 (2005) 740–770.

W.W. Powell, and K. Snellman, "The Knowledge Economy," *Annual Review of Sociology* 30: 1 (2004) 199–220.

A. Power, J. Ploger, and A. Winkler, *Phoenix Cities: The Fall and Rise of Great Industrial Cities* (Bristol: The Policy Press, 2010).

A.C. Pratt, "Creative Cities: the Cultural Industries and the Creative Class," *Geografiska Annaler: Series B, Human Geography* 90: 2 (2008) 107–117.

A.C. Pratt, "Urban Regeneration: From the Arts 'Feel Good' Factor to the Cultural Economy. A Case Study of Hoxton, London," *Urban Studies* 46: 5-6 (2009) 1041–1061.

A.C. Pratt, "The Cultural Contradictions of the Creative City," *Culture and Society* 2 (2011) 123–130.

C. Rabari, and M. Storper, "The Digital Skin of Cities: Urban Theory and Research in the age of the Sensored and Metered City, Ubiquitous Computing and big Data," *Cambridge Journal of Regions Economy and Society* 8: 1 (2015) 27–42.

C. Ranci, *Milano e Le Città D'Europa Tra Competitività e Disuguaglianze* (Santarcangelo di Romagna: Maggioli, 2009).

C. Ranci, *Città Nella Rete Globale. Competitività e Disuguaglianze in Sei Città Europee* (Milano: Bruno Mondadori, 2010).

Regione Lombardia, Geoportale 2014, available at http://www.geoportale.regione.lombardia.it/ (accessed December 2015).

H. Rittel, and M. Webber, "Dilemmas in A General Theory of Planning," *Policy Sciences* 4: 2 (1973) 155–169.

E. Rivetti, *The Whispered Directory of Craftsmanship. A Contemporary Guide to the Italian Hand Making Ability* (Milano: Mondadori-Electa, 2013).

J. Robinson, "'Arriving At' Urban Policies: The Topological Spaces of Urban Policy Mobility," *International Journal of Urban and Regional Research* 39: 4 (2015) 831–834.

S. Roodhouse, *Cultural Quarters: Principles and Practices* (Bristol: Intellect, 2006).

E. Rullani, "L'economia Della Conoscenza e Il Lavoro Che Innova," in Butera F., Bagnara S., Cesaria R., Di Guardo S., eds., *Knowledge Working. Lavoro, Lavoratori, Società Della Conoscenza* (Milano: Mondadori, 2008) 165–184.

P.L. Sacco, and G. Ferilli, "Il Distretto Culturale Evoluto Nell'economia Post-Industriale" *Working Paper DADI, IUAV* 4:06 (Venezia, 2006).

W. Santagata, "Cultural District, Property Rights and Sustainable Economic Growth", *Working Paper EBLA Center* 01 (2002).

A.J. Scott, *The Cultural Economy of Cities* (London: Sage, 2000).

A.J. Scott, "Creative Cities: Conceptual Issues and Policy Questions," *Journal of Urban Affairs* 28: 1 (2006) 1–17.

A.J. Scott, *A World in Emergence. Cities and Regions in the 21st Century* (Northampton: Edward Elgar, 2012).

G. Semi, *Gentrification. Tutte le città come Disneyland?* (Il Mulino, Bologna, 2015).

R. Sennett, "No One Likes a City That's Too Smart," *The Guardian* December: 4 (2012).

R. Shearmur, "Are Cities the Font of Innovation? A Critical Review of the Literature on Cities and Innovation," *Cities* 29: 2 (2012) 9–18.

T. Shelton, M. Zook, and A. Wiig, "The Actually Existing Smart City," *Cambridge Journal of Regions, Economy and Society* 8: (2015) 13–25.

M. Storper, and A.J. Venables, "Buzz: Face-to-Face Contact and the Urban Economy," *Journal of Economic Geography* 4: 4 (2004) 351–370.

M. Storper, *Keys to the City* (Princeton, Oxford: Princeton University Press, 2013).

C. Tajani, "Milano Smart City è Proprio Milano," *Arcipelago Milano* 37: 8 (16 novembre 2016).

A. Vanolo, "Smartmentality: The Smart City as Disciplinary Strategy," *Urban Studies* 51: 5 (2014) 883–98.

A. Wiig, and E. Wyly, "Introduction: Thinking Through the Politics of Smart City," *Urban Geography* 37: 4 (2016) 485–493.

S. Zukin: *The Cultures of Cities* (Cambridge, MA: Blackwell, 1995).

S. Zukin, *Loft Living. Culture and Capital in Urban Change* (Baltimore and London: The Johns Hopkins University Press, 1982).

Co-working Spaces in Milan: Location Patterns and Urban Effects

Ilaria Mariotti, Carolina Pacchi, and Stefano Di Vita

ABSTRACT
The present paper investigates the location patterns and the effects co-working spaces generate on the urban context, issues that have been neglected by the existing literature. The focus is on Milan, the core of the Italian knowledge-based, creative, digital, and sharing economy, and the city hosting the largest number of co-working spaces in Italy. The paper addresses three main questions: (1) Where are the main locations of co-working spaces in Milan? (2) Are there any transformative effects of co-working spaces, respectively at the urban scale and at the very local scale? (3) What are their impacts in terms of spatial transformation and in terms of innovation in practices (for instance, work, leisure, or culture)? Desk research showed that location patterns of co-working spaces resemble those of service industries in urban areas, with a propinquity to the so-called "creative clusters." Field research shed light on urban effects, such as the participation of workers in co-working spaces in local community initiatives, their contribution to urban revitalization trends, and micro-scale physical transformations. The paper, therefore, helps to fill the gap in the literature about the location patterns of these new working spaces and their urban effects at different scales, both in terms of urban spaces and practices.

Introduction

Digital economies have fostered both dispersion and concentration of economic activities. Thanks to telecomputing technologies, and the ubiquitous access to dematerialized information and data provided by wireless, mobile telecommunications, and cloud computing, there has been a decoupling of workers and fixed job locations (Bizzarri, 2010), even though knowledge-based, digital, and creative jobs still tend to concentrate within large urban areas (Florida, 2005).

As is well recognized, the development of information and communication technologies has massively reduced the transaction costs (McCann, 2008) associated with overcoming spaces and multi-locality, while the effects of the digital industrial revolution on the possible ubiquitousness and democratization of work, society, and urban space are highly disputed (Anderson, 2012; Isin and Ruppert, 2015). Moreover, while ICTs favor a high flexibility and hybridization of workplaces—including unusual places like libraries, cafes, restaurants, hotels, and airport lounges—self-employed and freelance workers still need social and professional interaction in order to reduce the risks of isolation (particularly high in home working) and to increase meeting opportunities (Johns and Gratton, 2013; Moriset, 2014).

Within this context the late 2000s witnessed a wide diffusion of innovative workplaces named co-working spaces (hereinafter CSs).[1] The first one, labeled "Hat Factory," was founded in 2005 in San Francisco by the computer engineer Brad Neuberg, and since then the growth of CSs has been exponential across the world, in parallel to the spread of the global crisis (as will be explained in the next section). CSs are regarded as potential "serendipity accelerators" designed to host creative people and entrepreneurs, who endeavor to break isolation and to find a convivial environment that may favor meetings and collaboration (Moriset, 2014). One diffused hypothesis is that sharing the same space may provide a collaborative community to those kinds of workers—such as self-employed professionals and freelancers—who otherwise would not enjoy the relational component associated with a traditional corporate office. Another is that relational and geographic proximity within these new working spaces may foster information exchange and business opportunities (Spinuzzi, 2012; Parrino, 2015). Although there has been an overenthusiastic interpretation of the growth of the creative class (Florida, 2002), the related highly individualized jobs are characterized by frequent nonstandard employment patterns (Cappelli and Keller, 2013), which offer a nomadic and precarious worklife (Gandini, 2015) in search of new forms of identification. Besides, even though there are risks related to a co-working "bubble" (Moriset, 2014), concerning their prevalent exploitation for branding, marketing, and business purposes, there are immaterial benefits of CS microclusters for freelancers and independent workers such as knowledge transfer, informal exchange, cooperation and forms of horizontal interaction with others, and business opportunities. These benefits might occur because of geographical, social, organizational, institutional, or cognitive proximity (Boschma, 2005). Accordingly, additional effects might concern the urban context: from community building and the improvement of surrounding public space, to a wider urban revitalization (from both the economic and spatial points of view).

While there has been much media attention to CSs, there has not been much attention to this phenomenon in the scientific literature, especially in the fields related to urban studies. This paper has two aims. On the one hand, the investigation of CSs location patterns allows us to understand where they locate and why; on the other, the analysis of the effects they generate on the urban context might highlight spatial effects and changes in practices (i.e., work, leisure, or culture). The focus is on Milan, that is the Italian financial and economic hub (OECD, 2006), and represents the core of the Italian knowledge-based, creative, digital, and sharing economy (Camera di Commercio di Milano, 2016),[2] thus being the city hosting the largest number of co-working spaces in Italy (MyCowo, 2014).[3] Specifically, the research questions guiding the analysis of the Milan CSs, are the following: (1) What are the main location patterns of CSs in Milan? (2) Are there any transformative effects of CSs respectively at the urban scale and at the very local? (3) What are their impacts in terms of spatial transformation and in terms of innovation in practices (for instance, work, leisure, or culture)?

The empirical analysis consists of two research activities. Desk research, carried out from Spring 2014 to Summer 2015, that investigated the location factors of all 68 Milan CSs (identified in July 2015), and field research on a selection of 20 of these CSs, which began in Spring 2015 and ended in Summer 2016. This research explored whether and how specific urban effects were revealed. The results of the desk research showed that CSs location patterns resemble those of service industries in urban areas (i.e., urbanization and localization economies; market size and potential; skilled labor force availability and business opportunities; transportation accessibility), and the so-called "creative clusters" represent a preferential location for these new working spaces. In addition, the low costs of premises as well as some "soft" factors (i.e., personal preferences of the CSs founders) play a role. The results of the field research shed light on the urban effects, such as the participation of "co-workers"[4] in local community initiatives, the contribution of these spaces to urban revitalization trends, and the micro-scale physical transformations of these spaces.

This paper is organized by following this introduction with a literature review that discusses the emergence and diffusion of CSs in relation to a broader context, including the development of ICTs, the growing of knowledge-based, creative, digital, and sharing economy, the economic downturn, and the novel role played by the several proximity measures in fostering interactive learning and innovation. The analysis of the CSs located in Milan is then presented. One section is devoted to the adopted methodology, and to the research questions that the empirical analysis aims to answer. The data used in this analysis came from two different sources: desk research (carried out in 2014–2015) and field research (carried out in 2015–2016). Mapping and descriptive statistics allow us to present the location patterns of Milan's CSs. The research outcomes regarding the urban effects of Milan's CSs, both in terms of spaces and practices, are presented in a discussion section. While these results seem different at macro and micro scales, we conclude with policy suggestions.

The Emergence and Diffusion of the CSs Phenomenon

The growth of ICTs—such as Web 2.0, personal mobile devices, open source data, new generation printers—has been contributing to the development of knowledge-based, creative, and digital economies; that is, to the growth of the information society and the emergence of the "sharing economy." This has led to changes in the way work is done and in the places where it occurs. The related growth of knowledge of the number of creative and digital workers, as well as the consequent spread of co-working spaces and makerspaces[5] (Anderson, 2012), have produced various effects including changes to space (triggering urban regeneration), to the economy, and to society (favoring knowledge transfer, informal exchange, interaction, and collaboration). ICTs can be seen as significant drivers of spatial, economic, and social changes, and can contribute to shifting place-based mass production to global, flexible, and knowledge-based organizations (Fernández Maldonado, 2012). The challenge of the twenty-first century is the resumption of productivity (Guallart, 2012), albeit in new and more specialized forms mixing manufacturing and services, now difficult to distinguish. The recent advances in ICTs have, indeed, fostered not only transmissions of information, but also new interactions among users, with a consequent boom in shared production and consumption (Ratti and Claudel, 2015) of goods, services, ideas, skills, and time. This represents the above mentioned shift from centralized models of resource management in industrial societies (from large-scale production centers to small-scale individual consumers) to distributed models in information society (connecting people with people, objects with objects, buildings with buildings, or communities with communities) (Guallart, 2012). In Western countries, in particular, the crisis of traditional manufacturing in the 1970s, on the one hand, and the recent and ongoing effects of the world financial crisis and global economic downturn, on the other, have stimulated the growth of innovative economies, for which ICTs are fundamental requirements (Rifkin, 2011).

Within this context, makerspaces like fabrication laboratories (Fab-Labs) transform digital data into physical objects (and *vice versa*) through their digital fabrication machines, favoring both the development of specialized productions (locally oriented) and the empowerment of users (Gershenfeld, 2012; Guallart, 2012). Besides, co-working spaces integrate knowledge, creative, and digital workers (Moriset, 2014), and their geographical proximity and non-hierarchical relationships, which are typical of collaborative communities, may generate socialization and, consequently, business opportunities (Spinuzzi, 2012). The exchange of tacit knowledge still requires face-to-face contacts, which may be frequent in the case of co-location (as it happens in CSs), or episodic by bringing people together through travel now and then (McCann, 2008). While codified knowledge can be exchanged at a distance, tacit knowledge (that includes social and cultural components) requires an intimate trust between participants, achievable only through close and direct contact among individuals (Moriset, 2014). Besides, "face-to-face contacts support serendipitous knowledge, and most importantly, stimulate and strengthen other forms of proximity pivotal in enabling knowledge exchange within organizations" (Parrino, 2015: 3). The Evolutionary Economic Geography framework (Boschma, 2005) has highlighted, indeed, that the impact of geographical proximity on interactive learning and innovation should always be examined in relation to other dimensions of proximity itself (i.e., organizational and cognitive). "The need for geographical proximity is rather weak when there is a clear division of precise tasks that are coordinated by a strong central authority (organizational proximity), and the partners share the same cognitive experience (cognitive proximity)" (Boschma, 2005: 69). Nevertheless, "geographical proximity may play a complementary role in building and strengthening social, organizational, institutional, and cognitive proximity" (Boschma, 2005: 70).

While telecenters, business centers, and incubators often provide co-working spaces, and although there is increasing flexibility and hybridization of workplaces and work practices, real CSs should be totally dedicated to co-working activities by offering openness, collaboration, accessibility, and community (Moriset, 2014). It means that co-working should be first "an atmosphere, a spirit, and even a lifestyle" (Moriset, 2014: 7), and that co-workers should not be just (often precarious) professionals, but professionals aiming at increasing their business through the nurturing of social relations, as well as the establishment of temporary partnerships and collaborations (Spinuzzi, 2012). CSs should not only be characterized by an open-source approach to working (Lange, 2011), but by a new type of employment and organization, based on the value production's socialization (Gandini, 2015). A CS should, therefore, be considered as a "relational milieu" (Gandini, 2015: 200), which may be able to provide the necessary physical and relational intermediation to networking activities (Capdevila, 2013) required by (self-employed and freelance) knowledge, creative, and digital workers. On the one hand, this may allow the increase of their personal reputations, which differ from the old ways of job access, such as family ties (Colleoni and Ardvisson, 2014); on the other hand, this may allow the improvement of their social interactions and market positions (Gandini, 2015).

The growth of CSs in the last few years has been exponential across the world. Their annual increase was nearly 100 percent between 2007 and 2012, while Deskwanted[6]—a global network of co-working spaces and shared offices—reported nearly 2,500 CSs worldwide in 2013 and 7,800 CSs worldwide in 2015 (Foertsch, 2015), the outlook being a figure around 10,000 CSs worldwide by the end of 2016 (Foertsch, 2016). The development of co-working spaces has been particularly intense during and after the breaking out of the global crisis in 2008, beginning in dynamic cities such as Boston, San Francisco, and New York City in the United States, as well as Amsterdam, Barcelona, Berlin, London, and Paris in the European Union.[7] Therefore, CSs are located all over the world, with a prevalence for creative cities of advanced economies, characterized by high urban liveliness, vibrancy, and cosmopolitan milieu, attractive for knowledge, creative, and digital workers (Moriset, 2014). Cities are the focal points of innovation, the place where co-locating firms enjoy the presence of other creative companies, specialized in different industries and cross-fertilizing ideas through formal and informal exchange of information (Caragliu et al., 2016; Van Winden and Carvalho, 2016).

That growth was especially noticeable in South European countries, in which the property value collapse created a strong economic downturn. In this context, the growth of CSs seems related, on the one hand, to the need to reduce unemployment and, on the other, to the post-crisis availability of cheap office spaces (Moriset, 2014). However, most CSs (nearly 60 percent) are still not profitable. Generally, the most profitable are the largest ones, but the rescaling of existing co-working spaces is not always possible, and they often survive thanks to additional resources (such as public subsidies, service sales, or large firm sponsorships) (Foertsch, 2011; Coiffard, 2012).

Both as far as workers' welfare is concerned, and in terms of positive externalities on the urban environment, it is not possible to consider the effects of CSs as obvious and risk-free. Looking beyond the rhetoric of openness and cooperation, there are several issues concerning workers that are worthy of further investigation. First, there is the risk that such spaces become only a remedy to the precariousness and low profitability inherent in knowledge, creative, and digital production (Moriset, 2014), rather than places of real innovation and elaboration of new models of shared production. Precariousness and low profitability are very high for knowledge, creative, and digital workers (Gill and Pratt, 2008; Pratt, 2008; Grugulis and Stoyanova, 2011), and they question overenthusiasm about the creative class development (Florida, 2002). Consequently, observers have recently labeled these professionals as "lone eagles" (Moriset, 2014) because they are still not represented politically. Second, CSs risk becoming closed enclaves for an elite of high-skilled workers, rather than open opportunities for urban development, able to socialize the effects of these new models of production. Moreover, CSs intercept a loose work modality that is located between collaboration and cooperation on the one hand (in order to survive in a difficult working environment), and competition on the other (between small businesses which operate in similar specialization fields) (Gandini, 2015). As far as the urban environment is concerned, several doubts challenge the research activities. CSs risk being spaces that are insulated and cut off from the social and spatial contexts in which they are located instead of becoming spaces that could spark urban regeneration and community rebuilding. It becomes interesting, particularly from a policy perspective, to understand under which conditions this may happen.

Although CSs are well covered by media, scientific literature is rather scant, and up to now no evidence has been provided (at least to our knowledge) about the location patterns of CSs, nor about their effects on the urban context at different scales (i.e., urban revitalization, improvement of surrounding public space, community building at the neighborhood and the city levels). This gap in literature may be associated with the general rhetoric in favor of the CSs, originating from the assumption that these new working places are innovative and have a transformative potential *per se*, without any consideration about the direction of such transformations, and about their ultimate effects on the urban realm and on local communities.

Scholars who have studied CSs mainly belong to sociology, anthropology, geography, business and management, and economics. Specifically, sociologists and anthropologists investigate the impact of these collective working spaces on the coworkers' careers and work life, the innovative role these spaces have within labor policies, as well as the role of proximity in knowledge exchange (Jones et al., 2009; Colleoni and Ardwisson, 2014; Gandini, 2015; Parrino, 2015). Geographers analyze the phenomenon looking at its patterns, and at the role of public policies subsidizing them (Moriset, 2014). Scholars in business and management investigate the knowledge dynamics that take place in localized emerging communities in CSs; that is, on individual and inter-person environmental experience, as well as on job characteristics (Capdevila, 2013). Finally, scholars in economics focus on the coworkers' economic performance by comparing them to single self-employed professionals and freelancers, or to small firms (Deijl, 2014). However, until now investigating this phenomenon from the perspective of urban planning and design has been done infrequently.

Co-working Spaces in Milan: Methodology and Research Questions

The present paper analyzes 68 CSs located in Milan as of July 2015 that were identified by the authors on the basis of the following definition: "Co-working spaces are shared workspaces utilized by different sorts of knowledge professionals, mostly freelancers, working in various degrees of specialization in the vast domain of the knowledge industry" (Gandini, 2015: 194). We identified Milan's 68 CSs from a list of co-working spaces generated by the Milan City Council in 2013, supplemented by press reviews and websites.

From a methodological point of view, two parallel research activities—that shared sources, contacts, data, and information—were carried out. The first mainly aimed at understanding the characteristics and location determinants of CSs, while the second was mainly oriented to identifying their effects on the urban context. The first consisted of desk research, carried out from spring 2014 to summer 2015, based on the collection of primary and secondary data[8] about (1) CSs characteristics (i.e., location, sector, size) and (2) the CSs urban context at the neighborhood scale, to better understand their location factors. The main location patterns of these new working spaces were investigated through mapping and descriptive statistics. This analysis allowed us to speculate on the urban effects of CSs, which were investigated in the second analysis.

Information about the Milan neighborhoods was taken from the database about the 88 NIL (that is, the *Nuclei di Identità Locale* or Local Identity Units), in which the Milan municipal area is articulated.[9] This database provides interesting information on the NIL characteristics such as: size, density, employment, number of research centers and universities, population composition (i.e., age, classes, and nationality). Additional information on accessibility to public transport, provided by the local public transport company (ATM),[10] was also added (Mariotti et al., 2015a).

The second analysis was based on field research that began in spring 2015 and ended in summer 2016. In this part of our research, we collected and analyzed press releases websites and made on-site visits to a selection of 20 representative CSs located in different parts of the city. During these visits, we conducted in-depth, semi-structured interviews with the managers of the facilities. The visits included an analysis of the urban environment surrounding these CSs, the typology and the original function of the buildings in which they are located, an appraisal of the internal structure (i.e., open spaces, office-rooms, facilities for leisure time), an evaluation of the degree of physical openness or closure of each CS (visibility from the street), combined with an investigation about the career path, motivation, and actual engagement of CSs managers.

The analysis concentrated on managers because the aim was to understand the original intentions and motivations leading them to open up a co-working space (i.e., the downsizing of their previous activity, a change in career path, the discovery of this new model of workspace during visits in other cities), their choices in terms of selection (if any) of coworkers by sector or other criteria, the reasons behind localization choices (matching the results of the desk research). The focus on CSs managers allowed us to get information about their personal experiences and goals, considerations about the relationships they have with the local contexts, and their perception on the effects of the CS they manage on the urban area. The analysis of the urban effects of these CSs was based on the investigation of (1) their transformative effects, respectively at the very local scale and at the urban one, and (2) their impacts in terms of spatial effects and practices.

Therefore, the entire empirical analysis—made by these two research activities—had the aim of answering the following research questions: (1) What are the main location patterns of CSs in Milan? (2) Are there any transformative effects of CSs, respectively at the urban scale and at the very local one? (3) What are their impacts in terms of spatial effects and in terms of innovations in practices (for instance, work, leisure, or culture)?

Location Patterns

In Italy, CSs are mainly concentrated in regions with large urban areas (i.e., Lombardy, Veneto, Emilia Romagna, Lazio, Tuscany, and Piedmont), and specifically in the largest cities, even though notable exceptions exist in rural and less dense areas. In this context, Milan attracted CSs (Pais, 2012) because it is an urban area characterized by the most dynamic socioeconomic and spatial systems of the country (Pasqui, 2015), particularly within the sector of creative industries (Bruzzese and Tamini, 2014).

Three of the city's main characteristics that favor the proliferation of CSs are:

(1) Milan has a long tradition as a "self-governing city," a city in which the role of private actors (both profit and non-profit), as well as of higher education and cultural institutions has always been as important as that of Local Authorities in setting the urban agenda and in implementing urban projects (Balducci, 2003; Balducci et al., 2011; Galimberti, 2013)
(2) Milan shows, at the same time, an increasing trend in the demand and supply of economic and social innovation (Comune di Milano, Fondazione Brodolini, 2016)

(3) Milan has strongly reacted to the current economic downturn by exploiting its traditional economic and social strengths (such as its high levels of entrepreneurial activity and its social cooperation), and by integrating them with both ICT innovations and the related growth of the sharing economy and society (Centro Studi PIM, 2016). This has been accomplished through the (mainly spontaneous) rise of collective organizational alternatives to traditional workplaces (Colleoni and Arvidsson, 2014) where new activities are promoted by sharing spaces, exchanging expertise and, consequently, reducing costs.

For the first point, this context has also strongly influenced the private sector, in particular as far as bottom-up initiatives are concerned: in many cases, there is a blurred boundary between profit and non-profit activities, in particular in social and cultural sectors, and CSs seems to be a good example of this. The second and third characteristics are strictly linked to the innovation culture of the city. That culture promotes knowledge exchange with local universities; cooperation among local firms investing in innovation; and support for specific local policies promoted by the City Council.[11] Specifically, beginning with the 2011–2016 Municipal Administration, the City Council assigned public abandoned spaces to private initiatives aimed at developing innovative working places, and it provided economic subsidies for both co-working spaces and makerspaces.[12] Since 2013 economic incentives have been made available to support the activities of coworkers and to improve the spatial quality of co-working spaces registered in a list defined in relation to specifically established requirements (Morandi and Di Vita, 2015).

The rise of co-working spaces in Milan is recent. The first one was opened in 2006, with their "boom years" occurring in 2012, 2013, and 2014 (See Figure 1); in July 2015, 68 CSs were identified in Milan. As mapping showed, they are mainly agglomerated in the northern part of the city (Viale Monza, Isola-Sarpi, and Lambrate-Città Studi, which host about 67 percent of CSs), followed by central districts (Brera-Centrale-Porta Venezia, with 20 percent), and by south-western neighborhoods (Tortona-Navigli, with the remaining 13 percent) (See Figures 2 and 3). According to the articulation of the Milan municipal area into 88 NIL, the desk research allowed us to recognize that the main agglomerations in the north concern the Local Identity Units characterized by good local public transport accessibility, high urban density (in terms of inhabitants and firms) and functional mix, and proximity to universities and research centers (Mariotti et al., 2015a).

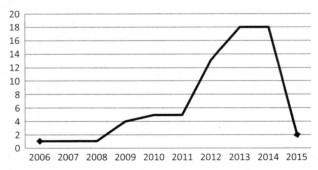

Figure 1. The number of new co-working spaces opened in Milan each year Source: elaboration by the authors.

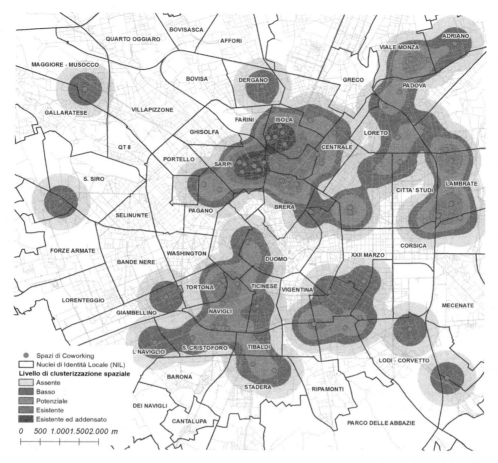

Figure 2. The density of co-working spaces in Milan (at July 2015) Source: Mariotti et al (2015a), p. 46.

Specifically, the first research activity compared the NIL hosting at least one CS with those not hosting any (See Table 1). This observation demonstrated that the location patterns of Milan CSs can be assimilated to the main location determinants of service industries in urban areas:

(1) the high density of business activities, that is a proxy of urbanization and localization economies, as well as market size and potential
(2) the proximity to universities and research centers, that is a proxy for a skilled labor force's availability and business opportunities
(3) the presence of a good local public transport network, that is a proxy of the degree of accessibility (Mariotti et al., 2015a, 2015b).

The comparison showed by Table 1 highlights that, on average, CSs choose areas at a larger distance from the center of the city, as it is proxied by the location of the Milan Cathedral,[13] to gain from lower costs of premises and higher availability rate of office spaces. Accordingly, they are located in neighborhoods where the number of immigrants is, on average, higher. Specifically, since high is the correlation between the availability of

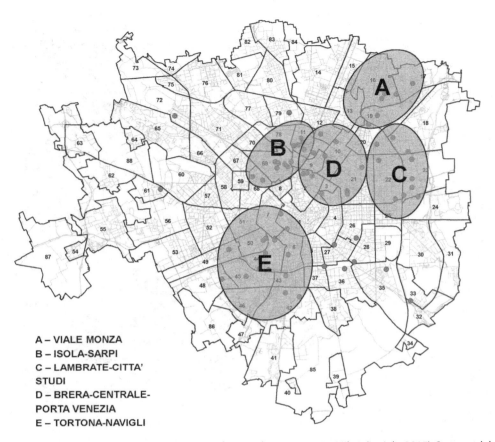

A – VIALE MONZA
B – ISOLA-SARPI
C – LAMBRATE-CITTA' STUDI
D – BRERA-CENTRALE-PORTA VENEZIA
E – TORTONA-NAVIGLI

Figure 3. The main urban agglomerations of co-working spaces in Milan (in July 2015) Source: elaboration by the authors.

Table 1. NIL characteristics and their attractiveness towards CSs

	NIL not hosting CSs				
Variable	Obs	Mean	Std. Dev.	Min	Max
CS	52	0	0	0	0
Urban density	52	6,491.363	5,983.118	6.377086	26,745.17
Jobs_2010	52	4,534.558	5,594.971	50	29,661
Uni_Research	52	0.403846	0.495455	0	1
Undergr_stops	52	0.711539	1.303638	0	5
LTP Accessibility	52	15.40385	16.98126	0	70
Distance from the Cathedral	52	3,832.361	1,784.915	520.0705	7,101.86
Foreign Population	52	2,206.038	2,617.346	0	12,721
Design week	52	0	0	0	0
NIL hosting CSs					
	Obs	Mean	Std. Dev.	Min	Max
CS	36	1.888889	1.389302	1	6
Urban density	36	11,786.98	5,743.859	337.6837	25,340.97
Jobs_2010	36	14,735.75	15,699.58	3,308	8,8291
Uni_Research	36	0.555556	0.503953	0	1
Undergr_stops	36	1.555556	1.747561	0	6
LTP Accessibility	36	29.52778	23.86089	0	100
Distance from the Cathedral	36	6,231.726	2,075.058	2,474.611	10,417.64
Foreign Population	36	4,153.444	3,395.069	309	15,708
Design week	36	0.222222	0.421637	0	1

Source: Elaboration by the authors on Mariotti et al. (2015a). Description of the variables is presented in the Appendix, Table A1.

vacant buildings, low real estate prices, and distance to the center, large-sized CSs (i.e., Avanzi-BarraA, Login, Monkey Business, Otto Film, or Talent Garden) are housed in former industrial and/or commercial buildings in peripheral areas (i.e., Viale Monza and Lambrate-Città Studi agglomerations). In contrast, the majority of CSs located in Milan-central districts (Brera-Centrale-Porta Venezia) are small sized and result from the "reconversion" of already existing professional spaces into shared workplaces (Parrino, 2015). Besides, all the NILs participating in the well known Milan Design Week[14] host at least one CS, thus highlighting a correlation between these new working spaces and the main creative urban districts (Bruzzese, 2015; Van Winden and Carvalho, 2016).

The location factors presented by these descriptive statistics have also been confirmed by the majority of the co-working managers who were interviewed during field research. "We wanted to buy a loft in order to enjoy more freedom in our organization, and this area was relatively cheap in 2011" (CS Manager 2). "The only consideration attached to the choice of the area was the accessibility to public transit" (CS Manager 1). Or "we first looked for a location near Bocconi University, which we thought could be a good source of people looking for a shared space, but we encountered some difficulties" (CS Manager 6). Nevertheless, it cannot be denied that the location of CSs within the Milan urban fabric may also be related to "softer" location factors: for instance, the personal preferences of the CSs founders, as well as of the coworkers, for that specific neighborhood, as underlined by the interviews of managers of co-working spaces.

In addition, this in-depth analysis of the 68 Milan CSs showed that about half of them are specialized in a specific sector, or branch of sectors, which may imply or not a selection of coworkers. The main sectors are: architecture and design (18 percent), digital professions[15] (10 percent), communication and information technology (8 percent, respectively), social innovation (5 percent) and other sectors (3 percent). Specifically, the CSs located in "creative neighborhoods" (such as the ones hosting exhibitions during Milan Design Week) (Bruzzese, 2015), focus on a specific activity. For instance, the CSs located in the Isola-Sarpi area are mainly specialized in the media sector, while the CSs located in the Tortona-Navigli area—that is, one of the most important Design Week districts—are mainly oriented to architects and designers. As stressed by the literature, the activities relying on symbolic knowledge (artistic and aesthetic) tend to prefer lively urban atmospheres (Asheim and Hansen, 2009; Van Winden and Carvalho, 2016) and, specifically, environments with a distinct and urban identity (Florida, 2008), like the Tortona-Navigli and Isola-Sarpi areas.

Urban Effects

As was mentioned earlier, one of the least investigated aspects of the diffusion of co-working spaces in contemporary cities is their urban effect, that is, the ability they may or may not have to positively affect the actual contexts in which they are located, in terms of community building (not just within the workspaces), improvement of surrounding public space, and ultimately urban revitalization. As the success of CSs cannot be taken for granted—there are high risks in the knowledge-based, creative, and digital economy (Gandini, 2015)—their growth potentials remain unknown (Moriset, 2014). The benefits of proximity in enhancing the diffusion of tacit knowledge within CSs cannot be automatically transposed at the neighborhood nor at the urban scale, but specific urban effects should be investigated.

It is quite difficult to derive specific criteria for this analysis from the literature on digital economies and the city, or on the relationships between the cultural economy and urban spaces (Pratt, 2011; Scott, 2014), because both literatures adopt a much wider perspective. However, we can certainly focus attention on the different scales at which phenomena manifest themselves, and to the core connection between spatial contexts and evolving practices (i.e., work, leisure, or culture). Moreover, from a methodological point of view, it is not easy to isolate the specific effects of CSs from the complex effects and externalities of other different uses and functions, especially in very dense areas as in the Milan CSs agglomerations, which have already been characterized by urban regeneration processes. Some emerging effects, however, have been identified, starting from those more frequently mentioned by the 20 interviewed co-working managers.

In order to critically interpret the role played by Milan CSs in the city (today and looking towards the future), and their transformative potentials, we used two interpretative axes: (1) one that moves from the very local to the urban scale; (2) the other one that distinguishes spaces and practices. From the on-site visits and the interviews, three typologies of CSs emerge as characteristic of the Milan case: (1) large, complex and (in some cases) hybrid spaces, hosting many seats as well as other facilities open to the internal and/or external community; (2) small, "office-like" CSs, offering just a few seats, often as a result of the downsizing of previous tertiary activities in professional fields (i.e., architecture, graphic design, accounting); (3) more mixed spaces in terms of both original intentions and dimensions.

While traditionally workspaces used to be closed, exclusive, detached from the urban environment, and in some cases utterly invisible, CSs (and, more in general, working spaces in the knowledge-based, creative, and digital economy) usually aim at being visible, transparent, showing what happens inside (Pacchi, 2015). Moreover, in the Milan case, an inherent tension remains: some CSs, notably the smaller and more "office-like" ones, are closed, secluded from other spaces, because they are devoted to a specific activity, and are sometimes invisible. However, larger CSs are more innovative, and they are more open to interactions with the urban context, both physically and in terms of uses, thus becoming more visible. While in the first case, the benefits of proximity tend, therefore, to remain limited to what happens inside the workspace, in the second case proximity dynamics can have spillover effects. Indeed, larger CSs—mainly settled in the north of the city in former productive or commercial buildings—are usually able to offer several facilities both to their coworkers (from meeting rooms to places of aggregation, such as kitchens, spaces to relax, or gardens) and to external users (e.g., cafés and restaurants), and they often organize events (e.g., meetings, exhibitions, seminars, or training courses) open to the outside community.[16]

Using the analysis of Milan CSs as an example, we identified four different quadrants for the inquiry (See Table 2). The first two quadrants concern spatial transformations and changes in practices of use at the urban scale; the remaining two refer to the same transformations and changes at the local scale. Even though the division between spaces and practices tends to be blurred at the phenomenological level (as empirical reality is complex and nuanced), it does, however, have an analytical value. On the basis of this field research, and thanks to the contribution provided by the desk research, the

Table 2. Synthesis of urban and local effects produced by CSs on urban spaces and practices

Scale/ Domain	Spaces	Practices
Urban	- Confirmation of central district attractiveness - Development of spontaneous aggregation in districts already devoted to creative and cultural industries, or previously characterized by workshops and handcrafts	- Contribution to the development of innovative services, mainly devoted to urban communities of freelancers and knowledge/creative/digital workers
Local	- Episodic transformations in the public space (temporary/installations or permanent/new equipment)	- Extension of daily and weekly cycles of use (i.e., evening and night activities, weekend activities) - Episodic participation in the strengthening of community ties (i.e., Social Streets) - Revitalization of existing retail and commercial activities - Strengthening mini-clusters of creative and cultural productions

Source: elaboration by the authors.

interpretation of the Milan CSs effects according to these quadrants is presented in the remaining part of this Section. On the one hand, one part of the interviews of the CSs managers was aimed at understanding which are the relationships between their CSs and the surrounding area, if there had been on their part explicit actions to strengthen these relationships and to root their space into the neighborhood, or if they detected any positive externality; the focus here being specifically on the importance of physical and social relations at the very local level. On the other hand, the effects at the urban scale are more derived from the interpretation of mapping and the location analysis, together with press releases and secondary materials on the evolution of CSs in Milan in general.

As far as the urban scale is concerned, the CSs main spatial effects are recognized in:

- the confirmation of the attractiveness of traditional and central commercial, business, and gentrified districts, such as in the case of the Brera-Centrale-Porta Venezia CSs agglomeration
- the development of spontaneous agglomerations formed by CSs and other innovative workplaces (such as makerspaces) in neighborhoods already devoted to creative and cultural industries; this is the case of the Isola-Sarpi, Lambrate-Città Studi, and Tortona-Navigli areas, which have been characterized by the diffusion and infill of these new uses during the last 10 to 15 years (Bruzzese and Tamini, 2014; Bruzzese, 2015)
- the development of spontaneous agglomerations of CSs and other innovative workplaces in areas of the city previously characterized by abandon and the presence of empty buildings formerly hosting workshops and handcrafts, as in Viale Monza area.

At the same urban scale, the main practices' effects of the Milan CSs are identified in their contribution to the development of innovative city services (such as the organization of dedicated events, or the growth of local, national, and international CS networks), which are mainly devoted to urban communities of—self-employed and freelance—

knowledge, creative, and digital workers. Events and services contribute to the increase of the traditional Milan attractiveness for local and international new workers. Periodic events such as the Italian and European Co-working Conferences (both held in Milan in 2015) or the Sharitaly Conference on the sharing economy (yearly held in Milan since 2013) show this trend.

While at the urban scale the Milan CSs effects are clearer, at the local level they are still partially uncertain, or difficult to be specifically identified within the complexity of other spatial and socioeconomic dynamics.

From the spatial point of view, they can be read in the episodic transformation of the public space, caused in individual cases: for instance, new urban equipment, space to rest or for leisure, art and cultural installations. This type of micro-urban transformation can be linked to the presence of new urban populations in the involved areas, triggered in turn by a new type of cultural and creative offer (such as readings, workshop, concerts, art performances, and exhibitions) hosted in the larger CSs, which are more articulated in terms of functions and services. This is the case of Login, and Talent Garden in the Lambrate-Città Studi and Viale Monza areas, and of Impact Hub in the Isola-Sarpi area. Such physical change can be permanent, but more frequently it is temporary, linked to the hosting of specific events: for instance, exhibitions connected to the already mentioned Milan Design Week. By the way, this may be an evolving situation, which may lead to projects designed to be temporary and becoming permanent, if the conditions for their use persist over time: "Since we frequently host events targeted at urban bikers, we asked the Municipality to have bicycle stands installed in front of our CS, but we did not succeed yet" (CS Manager 12).

Milan CSs can also modify the daily and weekly cycles of use within the districts they are located: for instance, sponsoring evening and night activities or weekend events in neighborhoods traditionally deprived of such occasions, such as the Viale Monza area, but in which temporary installations (like movable trolleys carrying "micro public spaces") are proposed. In the same area, the CS called *Unità di Produzione* temporarily offers a room to host visitors (which is also available on Airbnb). A different effect is then connected to the opportunity CSs may seize to contribute and participate in the strengthening of community ties at the neighborhood level. Finally, other local effects range from traditional services (such as forms of revitalization of existing retail and commercial activities, bars, and cafés), to more innovative ones, catering to the different populations who start using the area. On the one hand, the largest CSs (such as Login or Talent Garden in the Viale Monza area) have business discount schemes for coworkers in neighborhood shops and services. As one CS manager puts it, "this space contributes to the economic regeneration of the neighborhood, as far as cafes and restaurants are concerned" (CS Manager 4). On the other hand, as anticipated, larger and (in some cases) hybrid CSs—hosting, at the same time, co-working spaces, conference rooms, facilities for sports and leisure—are characterized by both more organized community-building activities inside, and networking with similar spaces in their neighborhood, thus strengthening mini-clusters of creative and cultural production. "Since we are here, the neighborhood is fast-changing: new CSs, makerspaces and a new type of retail are emerging, and this is creating a more interesting environment" (CS Manager 2).

Conclusions and Policy Implications

From the literature review and the empirical analysis, it is possible to come back to the research questions and to use them for further discussion.

In order to reflect upon the Milan case, we need to put it in perspective, reading the local and specific features of CSs diffusion in the city against a wider background. The Milan co-working spaces—which are mainly based on bottom-up initiatives (profit and non-profit), excluding (at least until 2016) direct investments of large corporate actors or public authorities—have rapidly become a recognizable system of places within the specific cultural and socioeconomic dynamics of the city. However, it is too early to assess whether this grassroots and small-scale dimension will be the characterizing element of the Milan CSs in the future, or if this trend will change as the phenomenon grows and becomes mainstream. Anyway, this current dynamic seems to be context-specific, since in other cities and countries large multinational companies (mainly high-tech such as Google and Microsoft), real estate developers, and national ICT companies have already been investing in CSs to improve their public profile and to experiment with open innovation, by infiltrating local entrepreneurial ecosystems in order to better feel market needs and monitor bottom up innovations (Moriset, 2014).

However, also in Milan larger CSs, promoted by more structured firms, have recently opened. One, CS *Copernico 38*, located in a big private building (near the CBD), that in the past was rented by the headquarters of regional public companies, was recently transformed to host 1,200 coworkers. Another space, *Talent Garden Calabiana*, located in the southeast urban regeneration area of Porta Romana has been recently transformed into an innovative and hybrid workspace, including not only a CS, but also a fab-lab. An operation promoted in cooperation with *The FabLab* by *Talent Garden*, an Italian CS company that is growing (more than others) throughout and outside the country, by opening up innovative workplaces in different cities.[17]

Also, the public incentives, which in Milan are relevant in comparison with other Italian cities, are still weak in comparison with other European countries. For instance, the Municipality funds to sustain coworkers and co-working spaces amount to €500,000 (Morandi and DiVita, 2015), while in Paris the only incubator, NUMA (which includes a CS) is supported by larger (both private and public) funds: €1 million from Google, €1 million from Orange, and €1.6 million from Région Ile de France (Moriset, 2014).

The empirical analysis allowed us to identify the multiple factors of CSs' localization and different types and scales of urban effects. Since Milan CSs specialize in services, their location determinants are: urbanization and localization economies, market size and potential, skilled labor force availability and business opportunities, and transportation accessibility. Moreover, additional factors play a role such as low real estate prices, former industrial buildings' availability, and "personal" considerations. Besides, CSs prefer to locate in "creative clusters" probably due to their lively atmosphere, and urban identity.

The face-to-face interviews of 20 CSs managers, together with the collection and analysis of press releases and websites, allowed us to detect different effects in terms of the ability to actually generate transformations at the urban and local scale. Specifically, the effects produced by CSs in their urban context are clearer at the urban scale than at the local scale. The ability of these innovative spaces to influence their neighborhoods and the city rests on their attracting new urban populations to those areas and then having socio-economic and micro-regeneration effects. It is still too early to analyze the spatial effects of these workspaces. Among the reasons why this is so is the longer time frame needed for spatial transformation and the tendency of CSs to recreate forms of public or common space inside their premises, rather than outside. The frequent cultural events that they host, their openness towards different users (not only self-employers and freelancers, but also students), their mix of working and leisure activities all call for the development of hybrid, innovative, but rather self-contained spaces. Therefore, this Milan CSs analysis shows that ICTs have been really affecting people's lives and jobs, but the actual relations between innovative technologies and new urban forms are still weak. That is, it seems to prove that, if the Internet has changed our lives, it has not yet changed our cities (Guallart, 2012).

The results of the present paper lead us to a final reflection about the possible role of local policies in strengthening the current trend towards more inclusive and shared workspaces, but also in socializing and diffusing their potentially positive effects at both the urban and the neighborhood levels. Even in the face of criticism about public policies supporting self-employment and freelance work—because of their high risks of low paying, short-tenured jobs, low value-added per worker, and little innovation capability (Moriset, 2014)—it is not possible to neglect their post-crisis potentialities. Without ignoring the risks of this phenomenon—such as the precariousness of knowledge, creative, and digital workers, the CSs low profitability, or the real estate speculation on this new brand—planners and policymakers of the new Milan Municipal Administration (2016–2021) should take strongly into account the general and specific features of the local CSs system. After the cycle of public policies promoted by the previous City Administration (2011–2016), different, but potentially integrated, strategies should be developed in order to promote a stronger and more resilient innovation environment:

- by emphasizing the bottom-up approach in the growth of Milan CSs
- by increasing public support through more coordinated, systematic, and strategically oriented public policies, for instance targeting innovative business models and the integration of a business and a local cooperation dimension, not only at the urban level, but also at the metropolitan one
- by involving funds provided by national-based big firms in order to obtain mutual benefits: for the support and development of local CSs and for the consolidation of market appeal and innovation capability of local-based big companies.

As far as the urban aspects are concerned, local policies should also facilitate stronger forms of interaction and hybridization between CSs and other initiatives in the field of culture and creativity on the one hand, and of social innovation on the other. These interventions should not be based on incentives, but rather on the strengthening of existing networks and on the creation of exchange platforms, aimed both at diffusing the possible cross-sectoral effects of the new forms of production and at lowering their risks of isolation and further social segregation. Opening up opportunities for temporary uses of new typologies of workspaces and putting them in contact with different urban populations may effectively result in a stronger and more resilient environment of innovation. For these reasons, the analysis of the effects of new working places on the urban context needs to be further explored.

Notes

1. Co-working spaces are innovative workplaces where independent (and frequently precarious) knowledge-based, creative, and digital workers--mainly freelancers or self-employed professionals--share their work spaces. They rent a desk (for months, days, or even just hours) in return for different kinds of services: both traditional (such as, for instance, administrative offices, meeting rooms, or spaces of aggregation) and digital (such as, for instance, wifi connections, or printers).
2. As an example, from January 2015 to February 2016, innovative start ups--characterized by high levels of technology and mainly operating in the fields of advanced services (information and communication; professional, scientific and technical activities; services for firms) grew by +61.5 percent in Italy and by +65.7 percent in Milan. This is an impressive phenomenon, even though the numbers are still small. Furthermore, within the Italian national context, Milan is the city with the highest concentration of innovative start ups (779), above Rome (450), and Turin (260) (Camera di Commercio di Milano, 2016).
3. Of the 285 co-working spaces in Italy in 2014, 190 are located in the Northern part of the country, 55 in the Central region, and 40 in the South. Within the Italian national context, Milan is the city with the highest concentration of these innovative workplaces (59), followed by Rome (23), and Turin (16) (MyCowo, 2014).
4. For our purposes, we define a "co-worker" as a person (one-person company or employee) working in a co-working space.
5. While co-working spaces are places where freelance workers share their working spaces and benefit from a collaborative working environment, makerspaces are dedicated to sharing the material production of objects. Therefore, they can be defined as places in which people meet to produce things in different domains. Among makerspaces, in the last few years there has been a growing diffusion of FabLabs, which follow the model of the MIT Fabrication Laboratory: they are places devoted to digital fabrication and experimentation. The relevance of making, as a new attitude towards fabrication, has been the object of extensive investigation (Anderson, 2012).
6. Website: www.deskwanted.wordpress.com.
7. Source: Deskwanted (www.deskwanted.wordpress.com).
8. Specific information about the CSs was also collected through telephone calls to CSs managers.
9. The 2012 Milan Urban Plan introduced an articulation of the municipal area into 88 NIL (that is, *Nuclei di Identità Locale* or *Local Identity Units*), which try to correspond to city neighborhoods.
10. ATM stands for *Azienda Trasporti Milanesi*.
11. The Sector *Economic Innovation, Smart City and University* of the City Council approved the *Milan Smart City Guidelines* and the *Milan Sharing City Guidelines*, which highlight the importance of ICTs as engines of urban change, and the meaning of cooperation and sharing economy for future urban development. On the one hand, by mixing and modifying traditional habits of producers and consumers of goods and services; on the other, by producing innovations in terms of economic growth, social inclusion, education and training, technological development, and spatial regeneration (Morandi and Di Vita, 2015).
12. At the same time, the Milan City Council has directly invested in incubators such as, in chronological order, *PoliHub, Alimenta, SpeedMiUp, FabriQ, Base, MHUMA*, and the future *Smart City Lab*.
13. As the Milan urban fabric is strongly radiocentric, with the Cathedral in its geographical center, this monument represents the very spatial heart of the city and, accordingly to the

urban functions located in its surroundings; its district also represents the main centrality of local cultural, economic, and social activities.
14. Design Week is a temporary fringe event taking place every year since the early 1990s within several Milan neighborhoods during the Design Exhibition hosted by the Milan Trade Fair.
15. This sector comprises community managers, social media content producers, and branding consultants (Gandini, 2015).
16. This information comes from both our desk research and field research.
17. Up to now, in Bergamo, Brescia, Cosenza, Genoa, Milan (via Calabiana and via Merano), Padua, Pisa, Pordenone, Rome, Sarzana, and Turin, as well as in Barcelona (Spain), Bucharest (Romania), Kaunas (Lithuania), and Tirana (Albania) (www.talentgarden.org).

Acknowledgments

The present article aims at disseminating part of the research and teaching activities recently implemented within the new Research Hub *Innovations, Productions, and Urban Spaces* of the Architecture and Urban Studies Department at the Politecnico di Milano. The authors are grateful to the editor and the reviewers for the fruitful comments and suggestions to the previous version of the paper.

Disclosure statement

No potential conflict of interest was reported by the authors.

Bibliography

C. Anderson, *Makers. The New Industrial Revolution* (New York: Crown Pub, 2012).

B. Asheim, and H. Hansen, "Knowledge Bases, Talents, and Contexts: on the Usefulness of the Creative Class Approach in Sweden," *Economic Geography*, 85: 4 (2009) 425–442.

A. Balducci, "Policies, Plans and Projects: Governing the City Region of Milan," *DISP The Planning Review* 39 (2003) 59–70.

A. Balducci, V. Fedeli, and G. Pasqui, eds., *Strategic Planning for Contemporary Urban Regions* (Aldershot: Ashgate, 2011).

C. Bizzarri, "The Emerging Phenomenon of Coworking. A Redefinition of Job Market in the Networking Society," in K. Muller, S. Roth, and M. Zak, eds., *Social Dimension of Innovation* (Prague: Linde Nakladatelstvi, 2010) 195–206.

R. Boschma, "Editorial: Role of Proximity in Interaction and Performance: Conceptual and Empirical Challenges," *Regional Studies* 39: 1 (2005) 41–45.

A. Bruzzese, *Addensamenti creativi, trasformazioni urbane e Fuorisalone* (Santarcangelo di Romagna: Maggioli, 2015).

A. Bruzzese, and L. Tamini, *Servizi commerciali e prodizioni creative. Sei itinerari nella Milano che Cambia* (Milano: Mondadori, 2014).

Camera di Commercio di Milano, *Milano produttiva. 26° Rapporto della Camera di Commercio di Milano* (Milano: Camera di Commercio di Milano, 2016).

I. Capdevila, "Knowledge Dynamics in Localized Communities: Coworking Spaces as Microclusters" <http://ssrn.com/abstract=2414121> or https://doi.org/10.2139/ssrn.2414121> Accessed December 9, 2013.

P. Cappelli, and J.R. Keller, "Classifying Work in the New Economy," *Academy of Management Review* 38: 4 (2013) 575–596.

A. Caragliu, L. de Dominicis, and H.L.F. de Groot, "Both Marshall and Jacobs Were Right!," *Economic Geography* 92: 1 (2016) 87–111.

Centro Studi PIM, "Spazialità metropolitane. Economia, società e territorio," *Argomenti e Contributi* 15 (2016) 1–103.

X. Coiffard, "Le coworking créateur de richesse?" (2012) <http://angezanetti.com/le-coworking-createur-de-richesse>.

E. Colleoni, and A. Ardvisson, *Knowledge Sharing and Social Capital Building. The Role of Coworking Spaces in the Knowledge Economy in Milan*, Report of Municipality of Milan, Office for Youth (Milan: Municipality of Milan, 2014).

Comune di Milano, Fondazione Brodolini, "Milan White Paper on Social Innovation. Accelerating Milan's local ecosystem for social innovation" (Unpublished Report, 2016).

C.M. Deijl, *Two Heads are Better Than one* Rotterdam: (Erasmus University Rotterdam, Mimeo, 2014).

A.M. Fernández Maldonado, "ICT and Spatial Planning in European Cities: Reviewing the New Charter of Athens," *Built Environment* 38: 4 (2012) 469–483.

R. Florida, *The Rise of the Creative Class* (New York: Basic Books, 2002).

R. Florida, *Cities and the Creative Class* (New York: Routledge, 2005).

R. Florida, *Who's Your City?* (New York: Basic Books, 2008).

C. Foertsch, "The 2nd Global Coworking Survey," *Deskmag* <http://www.deskmag.com/en/first-results-of-global-coworking-survey-171> (2011).

C. Foertsch, "First Results of the New Global Coworking Survey," *Deskmag* <http://www.deskmag.com/en/first-results-of-the-new-global-coworking-survey-2015-16> (2015).

C. Foertsch, "2016 Coworking Forecast," *Deskmag* http://www.deskmag.com/en/2016-forecast-global-coworking-survey-results (2016)

D. Galimberti, "Milano – Città Metropolitana :entre conservatisme et innovation incrémentale au-delà du politique," *Métropoles*, 12 http://metropoles.revues.org/4633 (2013).

A. Gandini, "The Rise of Coworking Spaces: A Literature Review," *Ephemera, Theory and Politics in Organization* 15: I (2015) 193-205.

N. Gershenfeld, "How to Make Almost Anything. The Digital Fabrication Revolution," *Foreign Affairs* 91: 6 (2012) 43–57.

R.C. Gill, and A.C. Pratt, "In the Social Factory? Immaterial Labour, Precariousness and Cultural Work", *Theory, Culture and Society* 25: I (2008) 1-30.

I. Grugulis, D. Stoyanova, "The Missing Middle: Communities of Practices in a Freelance Labour Market," *Work, Employment and Society* 25: 2 (2011) 342-351.

V. Guallart, *The Self-Sufficient City* (New York City: Actar, 2012).

E. Isin, and E. Ruppert, *Being Digital Citizens* (London and New York: Rowman and Littlefield, 2015).

T. Johns, and L. Gratton, "The Third Wave of Virtual Work," *Harvard Business Review* 9: I https://hbr.org/2013/01/the-third-wave-of-virtual-work (2013).

D. Jones, T. Sundsted, and T. Bacigalupo, *I'm Outta Here: How Coworking Is Making the Office Obsolete* (Austin: NotanMBA Press, 2009).

B. Lange, "Re-Scaling Governance in Berlin's Creative Economy," *Culture Unbound: Journal of Current Cultural Research* 3 (2011) 187–208.

I. Mariotti, M. Bolocan, S. Di Vita, and G. Limonta, "Coworking Spaces in the Urban Context. A Cluster Analysis for the City of Milan, RSA Conference, Special Session," New manufacturing, creative productions, innovative workplaces, and urban space, (Piacenza, May 24–27th 2015b).

I. Mariotti, S. Di Vita, and G. Limonta, "Una geografia degli spazi di coworking a Milano," *Imprese e Città* 8 (2015a) 39-47.

P. McCann, "Globalization and Economic Geography: The World is Curved, not Flat," *Cambridge Journal of Regions, Economy and Society* 1 (2008) 351–370.

C. Morandi, and S. Di Vita, "ICT, nuove modalità di produzione e processi di rigenerazione urbana. I fab-lab a Milano," *Imprese e Città* 8 (2015) 81–88.

B. Moriset, "Building New Places of the Creative Economy. The Rise of Coworking Spaces," Paper presented at the 2nd geography of innovation international conference (Utrecht, January 2014).

MyCowo, *Infografica sul coworking in Italia* (Roma: MyCowo, 2014).

OECD, *OECD Territorial Reviews. Milan, Italy* (Paris: OECD Publishing, 2006).

C. Pacchi, "Coworking e innovazione urbana a Milano," *Imprese e Città* 8 (2015) 89–95.

I. Pais, *La Rete Che Lavora* (Milan: Egea, 2012).

L. Parrino, "Coworking: Assessing the Role of Proximity in Knowledge Exchange," *Knowledge Management Research & Practice* 13 (2015) 261–271.

G. Pasqui, "Milano e il suo nuovo ciclo di sviluppo," *Abitare* 543 (2015) 74–80.

A.C. Pratt, "Creative Cities. The Cultural Industries and the Creative Class," *Geografiska Annaler: Series B, Human Geography* 90: 2 (2008) 107-117.

A.C. Pratt, "The Cultural Contradictions of the Creative City," *City, Culture and Society* 2 (2011) 123–130.

C. Ratti, and M. Claudel, *Open Source Architecture* (London: Thames and Hudson, 2015).

J. Rifkin, *The Third Industrial Revolution. How Lateral Power is Transforming Energy, the Economy, and the World* (New York: Palgrave MacMillan, 2011).

A.J. Scott, "Beyond the Creative City: Cognitive–Cultural Capitalism and the New Urbanism," *Regional Studies* 48: 4 (2014) 565-578.

C. Spinuzzi, "Working Alone Together Coworking as Emergent Collaborative Activity," *Journal of Business and Technical Communication* 26: 4 (2012) 399-441.

W. van Winden, and L. Carvalho, "Urbanize or Perish? Assessing the Urbanization of Knowledge Locations in Europe," *Journal of Urban Technology*, 23: 1 (2016) 53.

Appendix

Table A1. Descriptions of variables

Variable	Description	Source
CSs	Number of co-working spaces located in Milan at July 2015	Authors' elaboration on various sources and field research
Urban density	Population per square km	2012 Milan Urban Plan
Jobs_2010	Number of employees in 2010	2012 Milan Urban Plan
Uni_Research	Number of universities and research centres	2012 Milan Urban Plan
Undergr_stops	Number of stops of the Milan underground lines	Local Public transport company (ATM)
Local Public Transport (LPT) accessibility	The number of the main public transport lines, excluding the underground	Local Public transport company (ATM)
Distance from the Cathedral	Distance from the Milan Cathedral in metres	Authors' elaboration
Foreign Population	Number of foreigners residing in the NIL	2012 Milan Urban Plan
Design week	Number of NIL hosting events during the Design Week	Authors' elaboration on various sources

Hubs of Internet Entrepreneurs: The Emergence of Co-working Offices in Shanghai, China

Bo Wang and Becky P. Y. Loo

ABSTRACT
Recently, the Chinese government has announced the "Internet plus" national strategy to encourage the development of Internet industries, particularly "innovations at the grassroots level." Supportive government policies at the national and local level, and strong market demand have led to the rise of "Internet plus" entrepreneurs. Many of them are not setting up their own offices but are using shared or co-working offices. This study examines the geographical factors, reasons, and processes behind the emergence of co-working offices for these Internet start-up firms through on-site observations and in-depth interviews with the management and users at major co-working offices in Shanghai, China.

Introduction

The advent of the Internet has revolutionized the ways people communicate and fundamentally changed people's mindsets and lifestyles (Kellerman and Thomas, 2002; Loo, 2012). Through the Internet, a global system of computer networks for interactions and commerce has emerged. Internet industries, made up of Internet companies that use the Internet as an integral part of their business model (Zook, 2008) have experienced rapid development and played an increasingly important role in economic growth. The availability of wireless Internet services further enables people to access the Internet almost anytime and anywhere. China is the country with the largest number of Internet users. According to the China Internet Network Information Center (CNNIC) as of June 2014 there were 0.63 billion Chinese Internet users and 83.4 percent of them used smart phones to access the Internet (CNNIC, 2014). More importantly, there has been a fast growth in the use of Internet applications in all major areas of commerce, leisure, entertainment, information acquisition, and communication (CNNIC, 2014). Yet, the development of the telecommunications industry in China has been strongly regulated by the government (Loo, 2003, 2004; Harwit, 2005). The regulatory regimes have set the bar for entry into the telecommunications sector very high and limited the services that Internet companies can offer (Zhang, 2009; Loo and Ngan, 2012; Zhen et al., 2015).

At the World Economic Forum in Davos in 2014 and the Third Session of the Eighteenth National People's Congress in 2015, "innovations at the grassroots level" and the "Internet plus" strategy were highlighted by Premier Li Keqiang (Li, 2014, 2015).

The "Internet plus" strategy specifically aims to support and encourage the development of the Internet to boost the employment, service quality, and innovative performance of the country (Li, 2014, 2015). As part of this effort, the development of co-working offices (*lianhe ban-gong kongjian* or *zhongchuang kongjian*) has been encouraged by both central and local governments in China (State Council, 2015). The present study attempts to shed light on the emergence of co-working offices as hubs of Internet entrepreneurs from a geographical perspective.

Literature Review

In the knowledge economy, information and knowledge have replaced labor and capital as the key factors of production (Castells, 1996). Easy and equal access to information and knowledge, with the aid of the Internet, helps to overcome the constraints of space and the friction of (physical) distance. However, the Internet has yet to play its role in decentralizing the geography of Internet industries (Zook, 2008; Moriset and Malecki, 2009). Internet entrepreneurs, especially start-up firms, are mainly clustered in a few areas (Zook, 2008). In the United States, the success of Silicon Valley has largely benefited from the early involvement of Internet entrepreneurs; and in this process, access to venture capital has played a key role (Kenney and Patton, 2005; Zook, 2008). Compared to its Western counterparts, the high degree of concentration of Internet firms in China has largely been attributed to government policies and regulations (Loo, 2003; Zhang, 2009; Zhen et al., 2015). Due to the absence of major domestic venture capital holders/companies (VCHs) in China before 1998 (White et al., 2005), access to foreign venture capital was pivotal to the beginning of Beijing's Internet industries under the Open Policy (Zhang, 2009). There are many stages at which Internet entrepreneurs or start-ups seek capital, like at the seed stage (i.e., when there is only an innovative idea that warrants further consideration), the start-up stage (i.e., product development, prototyping, and market research), or sometimes the first round (i.e., initial commercial production). For VCHs, a number of strategies have been developed to control risk (Zook, 2008). It is not uncommon to spread risk by investing in a basketful of companies, co-invest in companies with other VCHs, and invest stage by stage when certain targets of each stage are achieved. Another strategy for VCHs is to invest locally. This enables investors to know these early companies better and be more involved in their development (Gompers and Lerner, 2001).

Throughout the process, tacit knowledge circulation has been emphasized as a key factor in building investment relations (Zook, 2004). In Polanyi's framework, knowledge can be classified as explicit knowledge and tacit knowledge (Polanyi, 2012). Compared with explicit knowledge, tacit knowledge is difficult to be codified or transmitted in symbols as words, drawings, or other technical specifications without knowing the subject. Instead, it can only be acquired and transferred through practical experience and close interaction (Polanyi, 2012). Based on this understanding, Lundvall and Johnson (1994) further outline a typology of knowledge including: know-what, know-why, know-who, and know-how. Compared to a broad knowledge of facts (know-what) and an understanding of scientific principles (know-why), access to social networks (know-who) and specific skills (know-how) are more tacit in nature and could only be learned through interactions (Lundvall and Johnson, 1994). In this case, geographical proximity helps to provide more chances for interactions between VCHs and Internet entrepreneurs. However, it is argued that personal relationships (or relational proximity) and networks of practice, instead of physical closeness, are more important in spreading tacit knowledge (e.g., Uzzi, 1999; Brown and Duguid, 2001). This is even more important in China where personal relationships ("*guanxi*") have been very important in explaining the success of Chinese businesses (Su and Littlefield, 2001).

Furthermore, it is important to investigate the factors of innovation (in addition to government spending, skilled labor, and infrastructure) in understanding the geography of Internet entrepreneurs. Recognized as the cornerstone of capitalist economic development, innovation is geographically "lumpy" because of its tacit nature and is difficult to circulate between places far away (Porter, 2000; Storper, 2013). Theoretically, geographical proximity has been highlighted in the positive relationship between industrial clustering and innovation (Porter, 2000). In the first place, geographical proximity helps to intensify localized productive linkages in facilitating interactions and linkages between companies, inspiring both mutual cooperation and competition, building mutual trust and sharing collective resources (Marshall, 1920; Fan and Scott, 2003). Second, geographical proximity helps to produce an innovative milieu in enhancing innovation through collective learning led by intense interactions between actors (Camagni, 1995). Last but not least, geographical proximity helps to facilitate knowledge spillovers by stimulating tacit knowledge circulation in various forms, such as learning-by-doing, learning-by-using, and learning-by-interacting (Porter, 2000; Simmie, 2002).

Nowadays crowdsourcing allows innovations in software and hardware to be both shared and free, and crowdfunding allows entrepreneurs to raise funds through online appeals and favors the growth of micro-enterprises and entrepreneurs, as well as self-employed and freelance workers (Anderson, 2012). In fact, these trends have already affected the office-property industry. Many leading firms in Internet industries (e.g., IBM) are engaged in reducing office space by implementing "desk-sharing" practices (Sundsted at al., 2009). As a shared working environment, co-working offices have become increasingly popular among mobile workers (Kubátová, 2014). According to *Deskmag* (2015),[1] the first contemporary co-working office was established in San Francisco in 2005; nowadays, co-working offices are still highly concentrated in leading "creative" cities such as London, Berlin, and Paris in Europe, and San Francisco and New York in the United States. Moriset (2013) suggests that the creative environment in these cities attracted knowledge workers and, hence, led to the concentration of co-working offices. Generally, the co-working office is seen as a "bottom-up" space created by co-workers who hope to get a sense of community and build collaborative networks (Lange, 2011; Spinuzzi, 2012; Parrino, 2015). In this way, co-workers seek not to compete directly with each other but to bring "social ties" back into their working lives (Clark, 2007). Co-working offices were created to offer not only physical working spaces but also supportive and productive business environments where creativity and innovation can flourish (Spinuzzi, 2012). Accordingly, many co-working offices with specific client groups began to appear, and some became invitation-only spaces that aimed at stimulating or incubating innovative start-ups. Hence, co-working offices can be seen as "microclusters" of small businesses, entrepreneurs, and freelancers where intensive knowledge transfer takes place (Capdevila, 2013).

Finally, previous studies on the geography of Internet industries have often focused on the regional scale, without considering the current trend of micro-enterprises or entrepreneurs at a local scale, e.g., co-working offices. Geographical proximity is widely recognized as important in explaining the clustering of Internet entrepreneurs, VCHs, and innovations at a regional scale (Kenny and Patton, 2005). However, entrepreneurship is a socially and spatially embedded activity and, hence, the actual relationships and interactions among actors, and the ways tacit knowledge is transferred are crucial in understanding the economic geography of Internet entrepreneurs. Compared to studies that focused on the regional scale, a close investigation at the local scale helps to delineate a clearer picture of actors' relationships and interactions, venture capital relations, and innovation environments. A cluster of companies cannot guarantee frequent interactions, localized knowledge spillovers, and/or innovations. We need to look into the structure and nature of specific companies (or actors) and intra-firm, inter-firm, and extra-firm relations within different institutional environments (Martin and Sunley, 2003). The following research questions guide our analysis:

(1) In addition to Internet entrepreneurs, who are the major actors in co-working offices?
(2) Why do Internet entrepreneurs use co-working offices? What value do these spaces bring to owners and users?
(3) What are the major activities in these co-working offices both for their users and non-users?
(4) What are the locational factors for co-working offices?

In the next section, our research methods are described. Following that, we investigate the nature and structure of actors in co-working offices. The reasons for Internet entrepreneurs using these offices and the reasons for the founders to run co-working offices are then analyzed. Finally, we use what we have learned to discuss the locational factors that contribute to the growth of co-working spaces.

Research Methods

Empirical research in this study is based on detailed and intensive fieldwork conducted in Shanghai in January 2015, which included 29 semi-structured, in-depth interviews of 60–90 minutes (including many open comments), and a two-week-long onsite close observation of the operation and activities of 15 co-working offices. We selected Shanghai as a research area because it is one of China's most economically successful cities. Shanghai has some of the most expensive office space in China (with an average of 9.3 *yuan* per day per square meter in the city center: Qiu, 2015). More importantly, as a pioneer in China's economic reforms, the central government has high expectations that Shanghai will make breakthroughs in "innovations at the grassroots level" through the "Internet plus" strategy. The city has emphasized the development of co-working offices for boosting innovative performance and encouraging an entrepreneurial spirit (Shanghai Municipal Government, 2015b).

Because our research required in-depth interviews and onsite observations, we focused on maximizing the quality rather than the quantity of the interviews. A list of co-working offices was first compiled, based on the results from an Internet search, choosing

"Shanghai" and "co-working office (*lianhe ban-gong kongjian* and *zhongchuang kongjian*)" as keywords in Baidu.com[2] in October 2014. The relatively short list of nine companies reconfirmed that co-working offices are only beginning to emerge in Shanghai. After making initial contacts, four out of nine companies took part in this study. They were, iStart (IS), People Squared (PS), Suhehui (SH), Innovation Works (IW). These companies ran a total of 15 local co-working offices and were rapidly expanding. PS and SH had already set up eight and five branch offices in Shanghai within only four and two years, respectively. IS and IW were founded in 2011 and 2012, respectively. Both of them were planning to set up branches. On average, each co-working office was approximately 2,000 square meters in area and had around 40 entrepreneurial groups or start-up firms as tenants. The demand for co-working offices in Shanghai is evidently increasing. As the manager of PS remarked, "I feel that we are always looking for new offices during our development."

In each selected co-working office, one manager was first interviewed. Then, the interviews of users followed according to our onsite observations and the recommendations of the managers. Because of the lack of data on the composition of users, we also tried to balance the diversity of respondents in terms of age, gender, occupation, etc. Each in-depth interview took from 60 to 90 minutes, and a total of 29 users from different entrepreneurial groups were interviewed. In addition to the interviews, we took part in various events of the co-working offices over the two-week period. The first-hand experience provided us with valuable opportunities to closely observe the actors' relationships and interactions.

To analyze the emerging spatial pattern of co-working offices, their locations were mapped at the city scale. In total, 15 co-working offices of the four companies and 14 others (collected via Internet search and through local knowledge of the interviewees) were successfully identified. Therefore, our survey covered roughly 51.7 percent (15 out of 29) of co-working offices in Shanghai. Major locational factors that are important theoretically and/or mentioned by our interviewees were also mapped. All addresses were identified using the application programing interface of POI (points of interest) in *Baidu* map.[3]

Actors in Co-working Offices

In this study, we propose a conceptual framework as shown in Figure 1. An "Internet plus" project is the common factor that draws together the key actors of the entrepreneurial groups, founders/managers, VCHs, and the local government. In each entrepreneurial group, there are core members who initiated and developed the entrepreneurial plan and took charge of the project from its inception, and non-core members who are usually recruited during the development of the project. The goal of an entrepreneurial group is to set up a successful commercial company eventually, through transforming an innovative idea into an actual commercial product and getting venture capital in this process.

Generally, users of co-working offices are young and hold a higher education degree. Among the 11 core members and 18 non-core members, the majority were male (63.6 percent and 61.1 percent, respectively), non-local, that is, their hometowns were not in Shanghai (63.6 percent and 83.3 percent, respectively), and had prior working experience

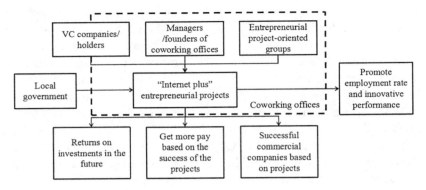

Figure 1. Actors and their networks in co-working offices

(90.9 percent and 72.2 percent, respectively). The high percentage of non-locals may be attributed to the local Shanghainese culture characterized as pragmatic (Liang, 2012). As the manager of IS added, "It would be unacceptable to families and friends for a local university graduate to give up opportunities to get a job from so many foreign enterprises and state-owned enterprises here in Shanghai." "For most local people, having a decent job with a regular income is more attractive than risking starting a new business," stated one local core member in PS. As the persons-in-charge, most core members (72.8 percent) had been involved in Internet industries for some time and had prior entrepreneurial experience. All members of the entrepreneurial groups were in two young age groups only (21–30 and 31–40 years old). Compared with core members (72.7 percent in the 31–40 age group), non-core members were even younger (83.3 percent in the 21–30 age group) but only 27.8 percent had entrepreneurial experience. As the manager of IW joked, "I usually call these users, 'male losers' (*nandiaosi*) who are young, single, and poor, but who all have a *Mayun* dream."[4] In fact, most of them had an optimistic attitude towards their enterprising projects (all core members and 66.8 percent of non-core members).

With an average of 59.5 working hours per week, these users worked very hard. Meanwhile, the Internet plays an important role in their daily work and life: as one member in PS remarked, "I am using the Internet almost every minute." Interestingly, though with the aid of the Internet these users could work at different places, only 8.2 percent of the working hours were spent at home or other workplaces. Obviously, this cannot be explained by limited Internet access because the services are actually good in most parts of Shanghai. Also, they used the Internet very often at home—nearly 3.2 hours per day. The distribution of working hours proves that the co-working office is their primary workplace.

It would be too simple to think that the founders/managers only want to provide a working space for rent. It would be equally wrong to believe that founders/managers earn their living mainly by the rent paid by the users. In fact, with an exception of PS (with an average monthly rent of 1380 *yuan* for a seat), the charge was much lower than the market price (Yicai.com, 2015). Specifically, the average rent in IS and IW was only 375 and 1200 *yuan*, respectively. The rentals collected from the entrepreneurial groups could only cover or partially cover the office rent and other daily operation costs of the office (e.g., salaries of managers and other staff, electricity, water, Internet service, and other utility fees). In SH, the office was provided free of charge (as told by the manager and also confirmed by users interviewed). The great variations in users' charges imply that the provision of office space and collecting rent from Internet entrepreneurs is not the primary reason for setting up these co-working offices.

Except for PS, the founders of the other three companies all had their own venture capital companies that mainly aimed at enterprises at the seed stage and start-up stage. In other words, they are VCHs themselves. In PS, the manager suggested that, "We have close cooperative relations with venture capital companies, and we are planning to have our own venture capital companies in the future." Therefore, the interest of the founders, similar to VCHs, heavily depends on the potential returns on investment. To maximize their returns, the key is to select and invest in projects with a high chance of success. For managers, they get more pay based on the success of the projects. For these managers as well as the founders, they have to attract more entrepreneurial groups with promising projects and help or guide them to achieve success.

Besides, all founders held a university degree or above and were veterans in Internet industries, with a rich background in Internet enterprises before setting up their co-working offices. All except one studied abroad and had working experience in Internet industries overseas. And it was the experience of participating in and learning from the business models of Internet companies abroad that inspired them to set up and run co-working offices in China. This is similar to the early development of Internet industries in China when the "glocalized" knowledge brokers played a key role (Zhang, 2009). Compared to the founders, hired managers were much younger. However, all of the interviewed managers had previous working experience and 50 percent of them had been engaged in Internet industries and had also tried to run their own business before.

In Shanghai, the municipal government has set the target of developing Shanghai as a "technological innovation center with global influence," and "Internet plus" entrepreneurial projects are seen as essential steps in reaching that target (Shanghai Municipal Government, 2015a). Accordingly, a series of local policies in encouraging and supporting entrepreneurial activities have been implemented to foster Shanghai's transition to a knowledge economy. The development of co-working offices was mentioned in the development strategies and planning of many local districts in Shanghai (Eastday.com, 2015). IS, SH, and IW confirmed that they enjoyed rent and service subsidies from the local government. PS, whose manager emphasized that the company did not receive any financial aid from the government, has propagated high-profile news on the visit of the Mayor and the Minister of Science and Technology over its media platforms (i.e., WeChat and website). Overall, the continual support from the government has effectively encouraged the other actors to expect the "Internet entrepreneur boom" to last.

Why Co-working Offices? The Potential Investment Relations and Knowledge Transfer

Though the financial returns to the founders/managers largely rely on the potential success of the businesses of the entrepreneurial groups, the investment relations are unspecified in most cases. In our study, with the exception of SH which offers offices free of charge with a contractual agreement,[5] there are no official terms on investment relations.

Therefore, it is uncertain whether the founders will invest in the projects of their tenants. Perhaps, the high failure rates of these projects with only an innovative idea or plan make it unnecessary to focus too much on investment in the first place. Nonetheless, it is the potential investment relationship that leads to the interactions between the entrepreneurial groups and the founders/managers. Through these interactions, the tacit knowledge of know-who and know-how are transferred among the founders/managers and the users, which may eventually lead to a final decision of the founders of the co-working office to invest in the start-up firms.

Usually, an entrepreneurial group is required to submit an enterprise proposal which will be reviewed by the founder, managers, and other professionals invited. The judgment is based not only on the project brief but also the group members involved. Through the project brief, it is easy to know what the entrepreneurs want to do, while it is difficult to know how they do it and who they are. And compared with the first kind of information, the latter two (especially the last kind of information) are the most important concerns for reviewers. For the project brief, "sometimes we only care about whether it is an Internet industry and whether the innovative idea is interesting," said the manager of IS. However, it is a long way from an innovative idea to an actual commercial product. And during the development, it is very common that the initial proposal will experience many changes. As the manager of SH remarked, "Usually a group comes in with an innovative idea, and comes out with another totally different product in the end." Compared with the unreliable future of an innovative idea, a reliable group becomes more predictable. As the manager of IW added, "Compared to lots of business opportunities for Internet entrepreneurs in China, which has the largest Internet market but is still at an initial commercial stage, there is a small group of reliable entrepreneurs who are our targets." Several rounds of face-to-face (F2F) interviews are mandatory for the selection in all 15 co-working offices. Accordingly, though each office has its WeChat and websites that recruit tenants, all of them regarded "introduction by acquaintance" as the most effective way to recruit tenants. This is consistent with our questions to users about how they knew the office, with 62.1 percent of all members and 90.9 percent of core members introduced and recommended by acquaintance or having personal interactions with managers/founders before. More importantly, these reliable groups will help to attract other reliable groups, as the manager of PS added:

> I insist that the principal thing for managing a co-working office is to gather (find or select) the right person or the right group in my office; nonetheless, in China, entrepreneurs belong to a narrow group of people who attract each other and thereby, the right person or the right group located here will improve our reputation and attract other right people or groups, just like the old adage "birds of a feather flock together" [*wuyileiju, renyiqunfen*].

Therefore, personal connections play an important role of transferring tacit knowledge of know-who from existing users to the founders/managers who, in turn, inform and help them make their choice of selecting a new entrepreneurial group. Meanwhile, personal relationships (*guanxi*) also play an important role in spreading tacit knowledge of know-who that helps to gather reliable and promising entrepreneurial groups to join a co-working office.

Second, in order to provide an environment for entrepreneurs to focus their limited time on their projects, managers/founders provide suggestions or undertake services including financial management, legislative services, media promotion, recruitment, market surveys, and company registrations. Especially for non-local entrepreneurs, acquiring the aforementioned services, which sometimes depend on local relationships, can be time-consuming. In addition, the concentration of users also enables managers/founders to fight for a better price and service quality when dealing with external service providers. More importantly, co-working offices are incubators as well. Managers/founders stay closely in touch with each group and are often involved in its entrepreneurial project, providing their support and suggestions which come from their own experience in Internet industries. In other words, there is an active transfer of know-how from the founders/managers to the users at co-working offices. Interestingly, unlike VCHs, managers/founders are more likely to see themselves as "entrepreneurial supervisors." As the manager of IW described:

> Enterprising activities are naturally never plain sailing. Entrepreneurs will inevitably encounter many unpredictable difficulties. It is useless to seek help from knowledge in books. Instead, these difficulties are usually solved step by step using the practical knowledge which, I think, could only be learned and accumulated by their own exploration or by frequent F2F interactions with experienced experts. And we are confident of our role as "enterprising supervisors" for these entrepreneurs.

In addition to participating in users' internal meetings or brainstorming sessions, managers/founders organize "entrepreneurial classes" almost every week in all 15 co-working offices. In a "class" that one of the authors attended, entrepreneurs, managers, the founder, and other VCHs and experts dressed in informal clothing (without ties and suits) communicated freely with each other during and after the "lesson." The frequent interactions between managers/founders and the entrepreneurial groups help them to know each other well and know the enterprising project in sufficient detail for an easy exchange of ideas. And during the interactions, a close relationship or "relational proximity" is developed. Of the core members, 90.9 percent confirmed that they received managers/founders' guidance and 72.7 percent considered the guidance important for their projects. As a core member in IS added:

> The founder of IS, with a good relationship with many successful entrepreneurs and VCHs, has a great deal of experience. He helped us analyze which idea or model was better and more promising in the market and whether the idea or model had been applied elsewhere and why this idea or model failed before. This kind of knowledge is very helpful for us.

Thus, it is the "relational proximity" coming from the frequent F2F interactions that helps to foster venture capital investment relations. Hence, a co-working office is not only a place for work but also for building investment relations through frequent interactions.

Group Member Interactions: The Co-Location of Group Members for Building Trust and Sense of Belonging

Interestingly, the relationship between core and non-core members cannot be easily explained by the employment relationship. Since economic returns will largely depend on a project's future success, members, whether core or non-core, are generally poorly paid with around 3,000 *yuan* per month. Most members (72.4 percent) were promised shares in the respective company if the project succeeds. A few members even got no pay. In fact, to a large extent, members are pursuing an enterprise dream based on their common project. As one lowly paid core member in PS remarked,

> Before coming here, I quit my job with a higher salary. But I have never regretted doing so because I cannot see a bright future in my former job, and I think I need to try new things and start my enterprise activity when I am still young. If this project succeeds, I will have a different career path, and I am looking forward to success!

Compared to monetary remunerations, higher importance has been attached to the entrepreneurial experience. Therefore, it should be noted that employment relations are rather loose in most entrepreneurial groups. In most cases, rather than salary, it is the project that bears the dream and practical experience that attracts and unites group members.

In spite of the loose employment relations, almost all members considered close cooperation within the same entrepreneurial group as needed (55.2 percent) and definitely needed (41.1 percent). And to work closely on the project, having better knowledge of each other (know-who), building mutual trust, and developing a sense of belonging are necessary. F2F interactions play an important role. First, it is noted that members have frequent F2F communication and their conversations are not limited to the work, with 89.7 percent discussing something besides work. As a core member in IS told us:

> During our working time and limited spare time, we will often use the open space (like, the café bar) and sometimes organize group activities (like, have a dinner and go to KTV) to have more F2F interactions. And we talk about almost everything, including our hobbies, past experience, something interesting. Through F2F interactions, we can know each other better and trust each other more. More importantly, we know we are "fellow travelers"![6] And we are in a group, working for a common project.

Second, the Internet took the place of in-person group meetings only 37.9 percent of the time and of two-person F2F meetings, 48.3 percent of the time. In addition, 89.6 percent of the members pointed out the importance of brainstorming. The emphasis on brainstorming is captured vividly by one core member in SH:

> Brainstorming enables our members to discuss one topic in our project in detail, and it helps us to know each other's idea better, which is difficult via telecommunications means. Sometimes we will make a decision together for the next step. Sometimes we get nothing and one may think it would really be a waste of time. However, I think this "waste of time" is still valuable for our group-building. Through brainstorming, each member gets a chance to share his or her own ideas that in turn give the person a sense of belonging. In addition, everyone is clearer about our project and knows each other better.

Generally, F2F communication and e-mail are adopted more often when discussing something related to work, while online social networking (OSN, such as WeChat and QQ) and F2F communications are used more often when discussing something besides work. Overall, F2F communication is stronger in conveying tacit knowledge which is difficult to communicate in any direct or codified way (Howells, 2002). Though e-mail has been widely used in dealing with working information, as many members confirmed, it is still hard to replace F2F communication. As one non-core member in IS told us:

> E-mail is mainly used to keep a record of our work for later reference. Usually we use e-mail to distribute tasks and then use e-mail to keep a record of the tasks. From the e-mails, you can

check each task. However, we use F2F meetings when discussing the task, especially when we encounter difficulties. Using e-mail would be rather ineffective.

Due to the importance and need of frequent F2F communications among group members, most (85.4 percent) preferred to work together physically in co-working offices. Meeting rooms in these co-working offices are frequently used. Despite the high demand for office space, managers/founders have never considered cutting down the number of meeting rooms. The provision of enough open space, such as café bars, gym corners and relaxation areas for entrepreneurs to communicate and interact is common in all co-working offices. Using the Xuhui office of PS as an example, it covers 2,000 square meters but has only 11 separate working rooms and 500 square meters of open common area.

Interactions Among Groups: Co-Locating to Form an Innovative Milieu with Cooperation and Competition

For managers/founders, cooperation among groups is highly encouraged, which can be easily read from their slogans (See Table 1). Every slogan conveys a sense of community. In PS, there is even an unspoken rule of the "knocking culture" that says that one should open the doors when the doors are knocked upon no matter who knocks. As the manager explained:

> Here, entrepreneurs use the same space. The concentration of excellent entrepreneurs enables us to build an entrepreneurial community. If each entrepreneurial group could share and learn from each other and help each other with an open mind, the rate of success would increase.

Furthermore, managers/founders organize regular activities open to all groups and some groups may be invited to demonstrate and/or discuss their projects. For instance, SH organizes "family night" every Wednesday. On a "family night" that we observed, the activity was held in a large meeting room and was rather informal (without banners, decorations, or even an event agenda). Any group was free to come out and show its work in progress. Managers, the founder, experts, representatives of VCHs, and other group members, wearing informal clothing, shared their comments. The concentration of entrepreneurs provided a good chance of receiving new ideas, learning from others, and cooperating as well. Of the members, 55.2 percent emphasized the "creative environment" as the main difference between a co-working office and a traditional workplace. The only regulation in IW is that no group should recruit a member of another group in the same co-working office without seeking approval.

However, the competition among different groups should not be overlooked. On the one hand, the competition propels each group to work harder. As one non-core

Table 1. Slogans of co-working offices surveyed

Company Name	Slogan
iStart (IS)	Mass entrepreneurs—fellow travelers!
People Squared (PS)	Pull down the "wall" between entrepreneurial groups and create a home for starters!
Suhehui (SH)	Help to translate your innovative idea into action and overcome the loneliness along the entrepreneurial path!
Innovation Works (IW)	Here is not only a place for incubating projects but also a place for different groups to share, cooperate, and develop!

member in PS added, "Once you notice that there are so many people still working when you are going to relax or leave early, you will easily feel the pressure." On the other hand, during interactions with members from another group, users are afraid that their good ideas might be "stolen." Therefore, members are discreet with the information they communicate, and the person to whom they communicate it. In particular, some key technology is protected before its commercial use. "Usually how much information I could share depends on how well I know the person and the relationship between the person and me. Of course, it also depends on how much the person would share with me," said a core member in SH. F2F meetings are more effective in controlling how much you want to share as the discussion goes along. Therefore, there is a clear drop in using e-mails when communicating with members of another group about something important or related to work (7.7 percent), compared with communication among group members (51.7 percent).

Locational Choice of Co-working Offices

In order to understand the geography of co-working offices, their locations and relevant institutions are mapped and shown schematically in Figure 2. According to previous studies, banks and other venture capital firms[7] are important factors in entrepreneurial clusters (Kenny and Patton, 2005; Zook, 2008). Given the role of government in the development of co-working offices in China, major government offices are also shown, such as those of the Development and Reform Commission, the Technology Bureau, and the Employment Service Center, all of which have been engaged in promoting "Internet plus" entrepreneurial projects. Moreover, given the close relationship among VCHs, entrepreneurs, and universities (e.g., Kenny et al., 2002), university campuses are also shown. We see that the pattern of co-working office locations is not "footloose" but is "tied" to local geographical contexts, including the location of major government offices, university campuses, banks, other venture capital firms, and metro stations. Generally, a substantial proportion of co-working offices (44.8 percent) are concentrated in the city center within the inner ring road, while most of the reminder are located in the pericenter in close proximity to a university campus or major government offices.

The concentration of co-working offices in the city center again proves that cutting down the rental cost is insufficient in explaining the development of co-working offices. The gathering of capital, talent, and information, and convenient public transport in the city center is critical in enabling these co-working offices to attract Internet entrepreneurs. Yet, no co-working offices are located at the most expensive central business district (CBD) of Lujiazui, with the highest density of banks and venture capital firms. In other words, though located within the city center/inner ring road, co-working offices tend to avoid the CBD where the rent is the highest. Unlike in Western countries, gaining some form of support from the local government is also important in China. In fact, IS and IW are located in buildings managed by local government offices[8] and enjoy rent discounts.

Apart from obtaining direct government support, collaboration with other institutions is also common. One of the co-working offices of SH, for instance, is located in an office vacated by Shanghai No. 1 Cotton Mill, a state-owned enterprise with plenty of space and funding. With the founder's rich experience in Internet industries, SH was invited to set up

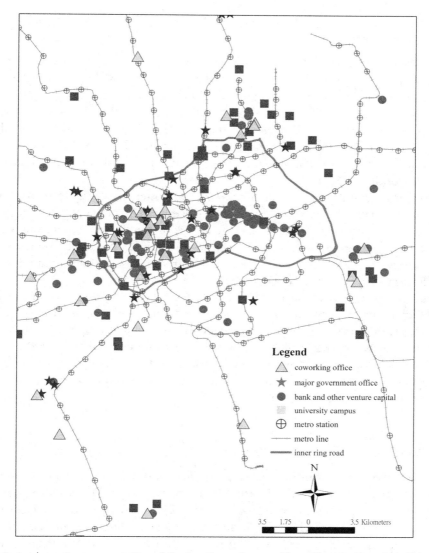

Figure 2. A schematic representation of the locations of co-working offices in Shanghai, China

the co-working office and given the responsibility of taking charge of the specific day-to-day operations. SH does not have to pay any office rent on the one hand, and it gets access to potential venture capital from Shanghai No. 1 Cotton Mill to invest in promising entrepreneurial groups, on the other.

Moreover, proximity to universities where young and energetic graduates gather is also an important locational factor. As the manager of PS emphasized:

> Always remember that the key factor of a co-working office is the entrepreneurs. What we need to do is to gather them and help them achieve success. And entrepreneurial activities are teamwork; the groups need to recruit new members during their expansion. And more importantly, these graduates, who use the Internet very often in their daily lives, have

plenty of customer experience and hold many interesting ideas that are important for entrepreneurial projects.

In fact, many universities have considered or already have begun to work with founders/managers of co-working offices in the hope of providing more chances for graduates to realize their innovative ideas/projects and encourage them to start their own businesses. As the manager of SH remarked, they have been invited to co-operate with Donghua University which has a good reputation in related disciplines. Using SH's experience and collaboration with Shanghai No. 1 Cotton Mill, they want to promote the integration of production, teaching, and research in their co-working offices.

Whether located in the city center or in the pericenter, proximity to public transport facilities, especially the metro stations, is a key requirement highlighted by all managers/founders and users. This is also in line with findings in other countries (e.g., Darchen, 2016). During the expansion of co-working offices, proximity to metro stations is emphasized because it allows the managers/founders to save time commuting among different branch offices and to keep their frequent interactions with all entrepreneurial groups. The importance of the metro has also been confirmed by users. For the early Internet entrepreneurs who are mostly not well off and non-local, they usually rent an apartment on the outskirts of Shanghai and frequently use public transport. Specifically, they spent an average of 46.2 minutes in one-way commuting, and 62.1 percent and 6.9 percent of them commuted by metro and bus, respectively. Except IS (which is 1.6 km away from the nearest metro station), all co-working offices are located within walking distance (within 500 m) of metro stations.

Conclusions

With the largest number of Internet users in the world, China shows great promise for entrepreneurial start-ups in the Internet industry. Supported by favorable government policies and strong market demand, co-working offices have evolved as hubs of Internet entrepreneurs in China. Through an analysis of the dynamics of the key actors, we suggest that cost savings, particularly in relation to rent, was not the major reason for the emergence of co-working offices. Instead, co-working offices serve multiple important functions, including building investment relations between entrepreneurs and VCHs, building trust and a sense of belonging among group members, and creating an innovative milieu characterized by "competitive cooperation." Because of the potential but unspecified investment relations, the tacit knowledge of know-who and know-how are effectively transferred through day-to-day interactions happening within co-working offices. Similar to the concentration of Internet industries in Silicon Valley (Zook, 2008), VCHs in China also play a key role in gathering entrepreneurial groups and founders/managers of co-working offices.

Generally, the spatial pattern of co-working offices is not "footloose." In China, support from local government is important and, thus, also influenced the locational choice of co-working offices. The collaboration with other institutions and the proximity to universities, which enable entrepreneurial groups to recruit new members and get customer experience, are also important locational considerations. However, whether located in the city center or in the pericenter, proximity to metro stations is considered very important for both managers/founders and members of entrepreneurial groups.

The development of co-working offices in China still faces many challenges. First, similar to previous studies, the important role of the government in shaping Internet industries is confirmed (Loo, 2003, 2004; Zhang, 2009). However, the relationship is complex. On the one hand, the founders/managers hope to get support from the government. On the other hand, they expect the government to stay out of the strategic directions and operations of co-working offices. Innovation sometimes could be regarded as a creative destruction of the old economic system (Schumpeter, 1934). In China, innovations brought about by successful "Internet plus" projects can engender challenges in government's regulation of the economy. Second, without a sound system of protection of intellectual property rights, the upsurge of the entrepreneurial spirit may be quenched. This is especially true in China's Internet industries (e.g., Wang et al., 2010; Zhen et al., 2015). Finally, it is worth mentioning that our research methodology, based on in-depth interviews and a limited number of case studies, has been shaped by the early development of co-working offices and by our research questions on understanding complex processes and relationships among different key actors. (See Figure 1.) Further studies on different types of co-working offices and their spatial dynamics will be important in understanding the processes and impacts of co-working offices and Internet start-ups in shaping the changing economic geography of China. In particular, are there different typologies of co-working spaces, maybe in relation to different locations? And is there something special about co-working spaces operating in Internet industries, as opposed to other industries? These are important future research directions about co-working offices in China.

Notes

1. *Deskmag* is one of the most comprehensive websites dedicated to information about the development of co-working spaces worldwide.
2. Baidu.com is the most popular search engine in China.
3. Similar to Google maps, Baidu map records the coordinates of each site which enables Internet users to query the addresses of these sites. A POI is a specific point location that people may find useful or interesting.
4. Mayun, or Jack Ma, is the founder of *Alibaba* which is the most popular and successful online-shopping website in China.
5. In this agreement, SH will receive an 8 percent share of the entrepreneurial project if it is successful in return for the free use of office and another 200,000 *yuan* fund.
6. "Fellow traveler" is a keyword in IS's slogan, (See Table 1.)
7. In this study, "banks" and "venture investment" are selected as POIs; and the latitude and longitude of 46 local headquarters of banks and 59 venture capital firms in Shanghai were eventually identified.
8. The building for IW and IS are managed by Shanghai Yangpu Human Resources and Social Security Bureau and Shanghai Minhang District Government, respectively.

Disclosure Statement

No potential conflict of interest was reported by the authors.

ORCID

Becky P. Y. Loo http://orcid.org/0000-0003-0822-5354

Bibliography

C. Anderson, *Makers: The New Industrial Revolution* (New York: Random House, 2012).
J.S. Brown and P. Duguid, "Knowledge and Organization: A Social-practice Perspective," *Organization Science* 12: 2 (2001) 198–213.
R.P. Camagni, "The Concept of Innovative Milieu and Its Relevance for Public Policies in European Lagging Regions," *Papers in Regional Science* 74: 4 (1995) 317–340.
I. Capdevila, "Knowledge Dynamics in Localized Communities: Coworking Spaces as Microclusters," (December 2013) <http://ssrn.com/abstract=2414121> Accessed April 12, 2015.
M. Castells, *The Information Age: Economy, Society and Culture. Vol. 1, The Rise of the Network Society* (Oxford: Blackwell, 1996).
China Internet Network Information Center (CNNIC), "The 34th Survey Report on Internet Development in China," <http://www.cnnic.net.cn/> Accessed April 12, 2015.
J. Clark, "Coworkers of the World, Unite!" *The American Prospect* (October 1, 2007) <http://prospect.org/article/coworkers-world-unite> Accessed April 15, 2015.
S. Darchen, "'Clusters' or 'Communities'? Analysing the Spatial Agglomeration of Video Game Companies in Australia," *Urban Geography* 37: 2 (2016) 202–222.
Deskmag, <http://www.deskmag.com/> Accessed 15 April 2015.
Eastday.com, "To Develop a 'Coworking Office" System in Baoshan District, Shanghai," (July 30, 2015) <http://sh.eastday.com/m/20150730/u1a8816480.html> Accessed August 18, 2015.
C.C. Fan and A.J. Scott, "Industrial Agglomeration and Development: A Survey of Spatial Economic Issues in East Asia and a Statistical Analysis of Chinese Regions," *Economic Geography* 79: 3 (2003) 295–319.
P. Gompers and J. Lerner, "The Venture Capital Revolution," *Journal of Economic Perspectives* 15: 2 (2001) 145–168.
E. Harwit, "Telecommunications and the Internet in Shanghai: Political and Economic Factors Shaping the Network in a Chinese City," *Urban Studies* 42: 10 (2005) 1837–1858.
J.R. Howells, "Tacit Knowledge, Innovation and Economic Geography," *Urban Studies* 39: 5–6 (2002) 871–884.
A. Kellerman and L. Thomas, *The Internet on Earth: A Geography of Information* (New Jersey: John Wiley & Sons, 2002).
M. Kenney, K. Han, and S. Tanaka, "Scattering Geese: The Venture Capital Industries of East Asia," A Report to the World Bank (Berkeley Roundtable on the International Economy, 2002).
M. Kenney and D. Patton, "Entrepreneurial Geographies: Support Networks in Three High-technology Industries," *Economic Geography*, 81: 2 (2005) 201–228.
J. Kubátová, "The Cause and Impact of the Development of Coworking in the Current Knowledge Economy," (May 2014) <http://connection.ebscohost.com/c/articles/99225223/cause-impact-development-coworking-current-knowledge-economy> Accessed on April 15, 2015.
B. Lange, "Professionalization in Space: Social-spatial Strategies of Culturepreneurs in Berlin," *Entrepreneurship and Regional Development* 23: 3–4 (2011) 259–279.
K. Li, "Premier Li's Speech at Davos Forum (2014)," <http://www.xinhuanet.com/fortune/zhibo/2014dwslt_zb1/> Accessed April 21, 2015.

K. Li, "Premier Report on the Work of the Government 2015, (2015)" <http://www.gov.cn/zhuanti/2015lh/premierreport/> Accessed April 21, 2015.

W.F. Liang, "On the Cultural Personalities of Late Lu Xun and 'Shanghai folks'," *Journal of Xuzhou Normal University (Philosophy and Social Science Edition)* 38: 4 (2012) 40–46 (in Chinese).

B.P.Y. Loo, "The Rise of a Digital Community in the People's Republic of China," *Journal of Urban Technology* 10: 1 (2003) 1–21.

B.P.Y. Loo, "Telecommunications Reforms in China: Towards an Analytical Framework," *Telecommunications Policy* 28: 9 (2004) 697–714.

B.P.Y. Loo, *The E-society* (New York: Nova Science Publishers, 2012).

B.P.Y. Loo and Y.L. Ngan, "Developing Mobile Telecommunications to Narrow Digital Divide in Developing Countries? Some Lessons from China," *Telecommunications Policy* 36: 10 (2012) 888–900.

B.-Ä. Lundvall and B. Johnson, "The Learning Economy," *Journal of Industry Studies* 1: 2 (1994) 23–42.

A. Marshall, "Principles of Economics" (1920) <http://www.econlib.org/library/Marshall/marP.html> Accessed April 27, 2015.

R. Martin and P. Sunley, "Deconstructing Clusters: Chaotic Concept or Policy Panacea?," *Journal of Economic Geography* 3: 1 (2003) 5–35.

B. Moriset, "Building New Places of the Creative Economy. The Rise of Coworking Spaces," (2013) <https://halshs.archives-ouvertes.fr/halshs-00914075> Accessed April 20, 2015.

B. Moriset and E.J. Malecki, "Organization versus Space: The Paradoxical Geographies of the Digital Economy," *Geography Compass* 3: 1 (2009) 256–274.

L. Parrino, "Coworking: Assessing the Role of Proximity in Knowledge Exchange," *Knowledge Management Research & Practice* 13: 3 (2015) 261–271.

M. Polanyi, *Personal Knowledge: Towards a Post-critical Philosophy* (Chicago: University of Chicago Press, 2012).

M.E. Porter, "Location, Competition, and Economic Development: Local Clusters in a Global Economy," *Economic Development Quarterly* 14: 1 (2000) 15–34.

G. Qiu, "Intensified Competition for Office Buildings in Shanghai," (February 2, 2015) <http://bj.house.sina.com.cn/news/2015-02-02/14395967903796423340091.shtml> Accessed April 21, 2015.

J.A. Schumpeter, *The Theory of Economic Development: An Inquiry into profits, Capital, Credit, Interest, and the Business Cycle* (Piscataway, N.J.: Transaction Publiishers, 1934).

Shanghai Municipal Government, "Building the Technological Innovation Center with Global Influence in Shanghai," (2015a) <http://www.shanghai.gov.cn/shanghai/node2314/n32792/n32874/> Accessed June 15, 2015.

Shanghai Municipal Government, "Guidance on the Developing Coworking Offices to Advance "Innovations at the Grassroots Level" and "Mass Entrepreneurial Spirit," (2015b) <http://www.stcsm.gov.cn/gk/zcfg/gfxwz/fzfwj/342869.htm> Accessed August 8, 2015.

J. Simmie, "Knowledge Spillovers and Reasons for the Concentration of Innovative SMEs," *Urban Studies* 39: 5–6 (2002) 885–902.

C. Spinuzzi, "Working Alone Together: Coworking as Emergent Collaborative Activity," *Journal of Business and Technical Communication* 26: 4 (2012) 399–441.

State Council, "Directives of the State Council in Developing Coworking Spaces and Promoting the Creative Industry," <http://www.gov.cn/zhengce/content/2015-03/11/content_9519.htm> Accessed November 30, 2015.

M. Storper, *Keys to the City: How Economics, Institutions, Social Interaction, and Politics Shape Development* (Princeton, New Jersey: Princeton University Press, 2013).

C. Su and J.E. Littlefield, "Entering Guanxi: A Business Ethical Dilemma in Mainland China?," *Journal of Business Ethics* 33: 3 (2001) 199–210.

T. Sundsted, D. Jones, and T. Bacigalupo, *I am Outta Here: How Co-working is Making the Office Obsolete* (Morrisville, North Carolina: Lulu.com, 2009).

B. Uzzi, "Embeddedness in the Making of Financial Capital: How Social Relations and Networks Benefit Firms Seeking Financing," *American Sociological Review* 64: 4 (1999) 481–505.

C.C. Wang, G.C.S. Lin, and G.C. Li, "Industrial Clustering and Technological Innovation in China: New Evidence from the ICT Industry in Shenzhen," *Environment and Planning A* 42: 8 (2010) 1987–2010.

S. White, J. Gao, and W. Zhang, "Financing New Ventures in China: System Antecedents and Institutionalization," *Research Policy* 34: 6 (2005) 894–913.

Yicai.com, "Why the Renting Fees of a Coworking Office is Higher than a Grade A Office?" (April 15, 2015) <http://app.yicai.com/4606185.shtml> Accessed April 15, 2015.

J. Zhang, "Industry Building as Contested Market Building: Knowledge, Politics, and the Rise of Beijing in China's Virtual Economy," *Environment and Planning C: Government and Policy* 27: 4 (2009) 632–646.

F. Zhen, B. Wang and Z.C. Wei, "The Rise of the Internet City in China: Production and Consumption of Internet Information," *Urban Studies* 52: 13 (2015) 2313–2329.

M.A. Zook, "The Knowledge Brokers: Venture Capitalists, Tacit Knowledge and Regional Development," *International Journal of Urban and Regional Research* 28: 3 (2004) 621–641.

M.A. Zook, *The Geography of the Internet Industry: Venture Capital, Dot-coms, and Local Knowledge* Hoboken, (New Jersey: John Wiley & Sons, 2008).

Why Knowledge Megaprojects Will Fail to Transform Gulf Countries in Post-Carbon Economies: The Case of Qatar

Agatino Rizzo

ABSTRACT
In the last two decades, resource cities of the Arab Gulf Region have been known to urban scholars and the general public for their extravagant, large-scale urban developments. These so-called megaprojects have allowed Gulf governments to both brand their nations globally and compete regionally and internationally with other global economic centers. However, as oil-rich Gulf countries have attempted to diversify their revenue stream away from fossil fuels, a new urban typology has emerged in their capitals to facilitate the transition to the knowledge-intensive economy. In continuity with previous research on megaprojects in the Gulf and Asian countries, we have called this new typology Knowledge Megaprojects (KMs). In this paper, by using as a reference point for comparisons the existing literature on knowledge developments in the West, we set to exemplify KMs in the Gulf region by analyzing the case of Education City—a large knowledge campus being developed by the Qatari government in Doha. One main result of this study is that KMs replicate the same shortcomings of other more mundane, extravagant megaprojects and thus are unlikely to provide the right urban setting to foster a sustainable transition to the post-carbon economy in the Gulf.

Introduction

The Arabian Peninsula is one of the harshest, environmentally hostile climatic regions of the Earth. For a great part of the year, it is characterized by hot temperatures (up to 50 C), dry winds, and low precipitation. Under these conditions, in the decades before oil exploitation, the most important sources of livelihoods for the Gulf's indigenous population were fishing, seasonal pearling, and sea-borne trade with other tribes facing the Persian Gulf (today's Iran, Oman, and the other Trucial States). From the 1950s, with the introduction of oil drilling technologies from the West, the economies of the Gulf started to slowly change in favor of oil-related activities. As a result of these changes, the natural (marine and desert ecosystems), physical (cities and infrastructures) and socioeconomic (consumption patterns) balance of Gulf countries has been altered towards rapid urbanization (Riad, 1981; Al Buainain, 1999). While the size of Gulf settlements was previously determined by the balance of available fresh water, geographical location in respect to both pearling grounds and inland trade routes towards other settlements, and political/tribal alliances to secure stable trade (Riad, 1981: 11), with the advent of the oil industry the importance of these factors declined and were replaced by the increasing use of energy and resource-based revenues to desalinate sea water, expand roads for local transportation, and build harbors and airports to connect these once tiny polities to the rest of the global community. The impacts of this rapid transformation have been far-reaching: apart from the physical transformation of the cities themselves, perhaps the most immediately obvious changes have been demographic. In the Gulf, the situation may be roughly outlined as follows (Nagy, 1998; Rizzo, 2013): cheap labor from South Asia (mainly from India and Pakistan) has been employed in the labor-intensive construction industry, while South-East Asians (mainly from the Philippines and Indonesia) occupy the lower service sector; Arabs from the Middle East have expanded the capacity of the government in education and the public sector, while Western-educated expatriates have provided consultancy services for the design, implementation, and management of the newly built, or soon to be implemented, infrastructures. In countries such as the United Arab Emirates and Qatar, four in five residents are transnational workers with South Asians representing the largest group. However, locals' attitudes to this burgeoning transitional community vary: the term "expats" largely depicts white and/or western educated men who are pictured either as a successful, international group of highly skilled globetrotters who support the country's aspirations for modernity or an army of usurpers of high-paid jobs that should be allocated to nationals (Nagy, 2006). The term "laborers" is deployed towards the low-income, unskilled international migrants (often from South Asia, East Africa, and South-East Asia) who, through an archaic visa sponsorship system common to the Gulf called "kafala," are at the disposal of their patrons and not allowed to travel or bring their families along (Mohammad and Sidaway, 2016). Gulf governments play a crucial role in strengthening these divides: while they tirelessly work to attract the first group to their shores with speedy visa processes, their use of the "kafala" system makes sure that the low-skilled ones remain a transient presence.

During the 1980s and 1990s, however, major economic changes linked to the de-industrialization of cities in the West have fostered, thanks to powerful organizations such as the OECD, a global shift to the knowledge-based economy. In 2007, Knowledge and Technology-Intensive Industries (KTIs) accounted for nearly one-third of the world GDP while 90 percent of global R&D companies are located in the European Union, the United States, and East Asia (National Science Foundation, 2010). These significant economic and political changes have been championed by the major global cities world-wide. In first-tier global cities such as New York, London, Tokyo, and second-tier cities such as Stockholm, Barcelona, and Brisbane, heavy industrial activities are long gone, replaced by knowledge-intensive industries. In recent times, these trends have come to affect economic policy in the small emirates of the Gulf too; here countries have launched a series of policies to restructure their economies to slowly but progressively meet the newly established international targets to reduce carbon-based development and increase their share of KTIs (Crot, 2013). Urban planning literature has argued that an important factor to facilitate the transition from carbon to KTI is the ability to attract and retain transnational knowledge inhabitants such as students, scholars, researchers, knowledge managers, and so forth (Yigitcanlar et al., 2007). Within this context, the internationalization of higher education (Altbach and Knight, 2007) and the increasing share of International Branch Campuses have been crucial to facilitate Gulf's KTI agendas. Gulf countries have built an impressive number of what we have called in this paper *Knowledge Megaprojects* (KMs) such as Education City in Doha, Academic City in Dubai, King Abdulaziz City for Science and Technology in Saudi Arabia, and Masdar City in Abu Dhabi to attract knowledge industries, workers, and universities to their countries. Ewers and Malecki (2010: 495) have suggested that importing foreign, high-skilled labor to Gulf countries is one of the main strategies in "leapfrogging" the current, resource-based economy. In no other region of the world is the KMs phenomenon more evident than in the Gulf region. This alone makes it a good reason to study this phenomenon. While we acknowledge that knowledge activities may coexist in a number of developments, in this paper, we focus only on those megaprojects whereby education and research and development (R&D) activities are predominant. Our aim is to link knowledge-based urban development (KBUD) literature with that related to Gulf megaprojects for we believe that, in the face of increasing competition worldwide, there is the need to explore the impacts of KMs upon Gulf urbanism. Our main research questions are: How does Education City fares when compared to knowledge developments in the West? and Will this knowledge megaproject favor or hinder the transition of Qatar to a mature knowledge-based economy? To answer these questions, we have structured this paper as follows: in section two, after briefly sketching the overall Arabian urban context, we will review the main literature on megaprojects, and outline our understanding of knowledge megaprojects. In the third section, we will introduce the methodology and analysis of the results. In the conclusions, we will discuss the findings and suggest an alternative strategy for a sustainable transition to the post-carbon, knowledge-led economy in the Gulf.

From "Instant Urbanism" to Knowledge Megaprojects in the Gulf Region

In the last decade, a number of urban scholars have attempted to sketch the impacts of rapid urbanization in the oil-rich capitals of the Gulf. Bagaeen (2007: 174) has described Gulf cities with the term "Instant Urbanism" to depict their rapid transformation from small port cities to sprawling urban areas as opposed to the long-time evolution of Western cites—from the middle ages to modern times. Other terms such as "Dubaization" or "Dubaification" (Elsheshtawy, 2010: 250) have got traction in the academic community to exemplify cities' emulation of Dubai's urban megaprojects. Lately a book project on mega-urbanization in the global South has stressed the unprecedented scale and pace of development that characterized neo-utopian projects in the Gulf and beyond (Datta and Shaban, 2017). Dubai's Palm projects (both Jumeirah and Jebel Ali) have inspired a number of sea reclamation projects in the Gulf such as the oyster-like development of The Pearl and Lusail City in Qatar; the theme park and F1 track in Yas Marina as well as Al Reem, Saadiyat, and Lulu Islands in Abu Dhabi; Al Marjan Island in Ras Al Khaimah (UAE); and the North Bahrain New Town project in Manama. While Cugurullo (2016) and Crot (2013) have deconstructed the Gulf's first eco-city (Masdar City in Abu Dhabi) to show its neoliberal rationale, Ponzini (2011), Koch (2014), Moser et al. (2015), and Rizzo (2016) have highlighted the undemocratic, neo-patrimonial agenda driving urban development in the Gulf, and Jackson and Della Dora (2009) and Ouis (2011) have problematized the symbolic meanings of megaprojects and their impacts on the Gulf's social fabric.

In the domain of urban development, Adham (2008) has suggested a useful framework to link economic cycles to urban development in Doha: he introduced the terms urbanity of "transition," "necessity," "modernization," and "stagnation" to depict the transition from the vernacular to post-colonial, oil-based urban development. Rizzo (2013) has expanded Adham's framework by adding a new development stage called the "Megaproject Phase" to characterize the latest urbanism in the Gulf. According to Rizzo (2016: 4) the "typical Gulf megaproject is government-funded and integrated urban development, characterized by a specific theme (e.g., ancient Arab City, Global City, Mediterranean Riviera City, etc.) and a dominant function (e.g., sport, business, residential, etc.)." The political-economic rationale of megaprojects is to support the Gulf's economic diversification to attract new residents and tourists by providing a confined, in many cases gated and patrolled, space that is exempted by the socio-cultural norms and economic regulations in place in the existing city[1] (Ponzini, 2011; Ouis, 2011). Megaprojects are such an important aspect of state-sponsored neo-liberal policies that Gellert and Lynch (2003), in their analysis of biogeophysical and social displacements caused by megaprojects in the global South, have introduced the typology "consumption megaproject" to differentiate these latter from infrastructural/industrial ones. Gellert and Lynch's (2003: 16) consumption megaprojects are "massive tourist installations, malls, theme parks, and real estate developments" such as the ones we find in Dubai, Abu Dhabi, Doha, and the rest of the Gulf region. The adjective "consumption" is indicative of the main functions taking place within this megaproject type: leisure, shopping, and exclusive lifestyle living. However, what Gellert and Lynch (2003) miss in their analysis is the important contribution that knowledge activities play in the agendas of Gulf's governments. Knowledge-intensive activities have been targeted by Gulf governments as a crucial aspect of economic modernization and sustainable growth. Launched almost 10 years ago, the "Qatar National Vision 2030" (GSDP, 2008) identifies knowledge as a crucial ingredient in sustaining economic development in the small emirate. For the vision, "positioning [Qatar] as a regional hub for knowledge and for high value industrial and service activities" would provide a "broader platform" for sustainable economic development when the oil runs out. Similarly, Abu Dhabi's vision (GAD, 2008) identifies the "sustainable knowledge-based economy" as one of the nine pillars for the future of the UAE emirate. Therefore, "[it] is vital for Abu Dhabi's involvement in this knowledge economy of the future that it has a world class telecommunications infrastructure and a population skilled in ICT techniques."

In this paper, we focus on education and research and development (R&D) facilities that aim at facilitating the economic transition of Gulf countries towards a knowledge-intensive economy. More specifically, while there is an established literature on the role of national university campuses in building knowledge cities (Yigitcanlar et al., 2008; Charles, 2011; den Heijer et al., 2012; König, 2013), in the remainder of this article we will focus on the nexus between International Branch Campuses (IBCs) and Asian megaprojects. In the past two decades, in emerging economies such as China, Malaysia, Singapore, and the United Arab Emirates scholars have reported the rising of the International Branch Campus (IBC) phenomenon (Cao, 2011: 8). An IBC is an off-shore, spin-off of, usually, a prestigious university (often based in the West) to provide education programs of international standards to students based in emerging markets in Asia. IBCs are simultaneously the result of the internationalization of the higher education market and the need for educated people to boost the economies of emerging markets (Altbach and

Knight, 2007: 290–291). Branch campuses are part of a new form of post-industrial urbanism that is inscribed in what Castells defines as "milieu of innovation" that is a condition that aims at "generating new knowledge, new processes, and new products" (Castells, 1996: 419). Knowledge-Based Urban Development (Knight, 1995) has been theorized in the West at least from the mid-1990s. In their *Technopoles of the World*, Castells and Hall (1994: 8) introduced the concept of urban areas that focus on "technologically innovative, industrial-related production [such as] technology parks, science cities, technopolises, and the like". Castells and Hall's (1994) "technopoles" are the spatial outcomes of three intertwined trends namely the globalization of the economy, the rapid development of information and communication technologies, and the rise of the information age whereby "productivity and competitiveness are increasingly based on the generation of new knowledge" (Castells & Hall, 1994: 3). While in countries such as Singapore the branch campus phenomenon is reaching saturation, in countries such as those in the Gulf, there is still room for growth (Cao, 2011). The number of IBCs in the Gulf is astonishing in many respects. A tiny country such as the United Arab Emirates (a bit shy of 10 million inhabitants) has more IBCs than China (See Figure 1) while Singapore (circa 5 million) and Qatar (circa 2 million) have more IBCs than Malaysia (circa 30 million) and South Korea (circa 50 million). When the total number of (public and private) universities is considered, the percentage of IBCs per country is even more interesting (See Figure 2): in early 2015 Qatar's IBCs represented 85 percent of the total number of universities running in the country while in the UAE this number is 66 percent, meaning that two-thirds of the universities in the country are IBCs. From the University of Southern Queensland, Murdoch University, Mahatma Gandhi University, Saint-Petersburg State University of Engineering and Economics, Heriot-Watt University, and Michigan State University in Dubai, to the University of Waterloo, Sorbonne University, and New York University in Abu Dhabi, to the College of North Atlantic, University

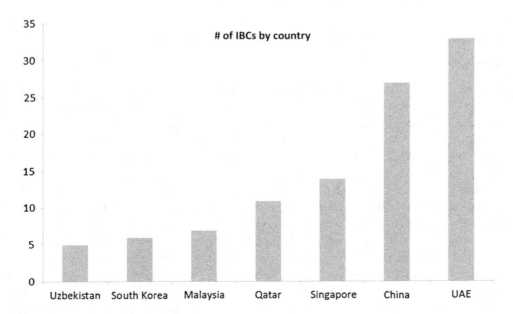

Figure 1. Top countries by number of IBC. *Source*: C-BERT, 2015

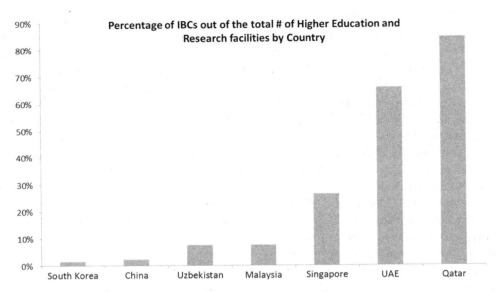

Figure 2. Top countries by percentage of IBC out of the total number. *Sources*: C-BERT, 2015; Webometrics, 2015

College London, Carnegie Mellon University, and Texas A&M University in Doha, Wilkins and others (2012: 74–76) note that the Gulf States have been the "largest recipients of transnational higher education globally, while Australia, the United Kingdom, and the United States have been the largest providers." Gulf leaders see IBCs as beneficial to providing much needed skills to locals in strategic sectors such as banking, aerospace, and medicine and helping to diversify their national economies away from oil and gas dominance (Davidson, 2009: 65; Peterson, 2009: 11).

The Case of Education City: Methodology and Results

Methodology

To explore the Gulf's Knowledge Megaprojects, we selected Qatar Foundation's Education City in Doha as a case study. From 1996, Qatar Foundation, a not-for-profit governmental organization, has worked to kick-start Knowledge and Technology-Intensive Industries (KTIs) in Qatar. Under the leadership of Sheikha Mozah bint Nasser, the royal spouse of the previous Emir in power (Sheikh Hamad bin Khalifa Al Thani), the Foundation is developing an area of approximately 16 square kilometers named Education City (See Figure 3) which, when completed, will include, 15 American and European universities, a major specialized teaching hospital, a central library, a convention center, an equestrian academy, an 18-hole golf club, large-scale on-campus housing, and a science and technology park. The project is located in the western part of the metropolitan area (See Figure 4), about 12 km from the old city center, in a previously inhabited area. Since 2001, new buildings and users (international students, universities' personnel, etc.) have moved into the area slowly replacing the previous residents (Rizzo, 2013). The choice to study Education City is not an attempt to generalize the characteristics of the many KMs currently being developed in the Gulf and Asia but rather to *exemplify* the main issues. At

Figure 3. In the center of the picture, Education City. *Source*: author's elaboration on Google Earth, 2015

this stage, we wish to raise questions about and explore the distinctive patterns of Knowledge Megaprojects (KMs). It is clear to us that the study of one case only is not sufficient to make final claims. However, qualitative, case-study analysis is an important first step in exploring issues and identifying directions for future studies (Shank, 2006; Creswell, 2009).

Education City will be analyzed according to an amended version of Yigitcanlar and others' (2008) model of Knowledge Precincts (KPs) in the West to reflect our interest in identifying the politics and processes underpinning megaprojects in the Gulf (Rizzo, 2017). The model has also been integrated with Gellert and Lynch's (2003) framework for studying social displacement generated by megaprojects. They (Gellert and Lynch, 2003) emphasize the importance of "primary" and "secondary" impacts: a primary impact is the one that is visible and immediate like the eviction of former residents while a secondary impact is less immediate, and more difficult to detect such as the loss or creation of new identities. While the primary impacts are an integral part of the megaproject process that is more predictable, the secondary impacts are an indirect consequence that is temporally and/or spatially less immediate and subjected to far greater uncertainty.

Thus, in addition to studying the "Program," "Centrality" (i.e., proximity, clustering, and access to services), "Branding," "Learning and Experimental Values" (i.e., activities that promote creativity and innovation), and "Social Connectivity" (i.e., face-to-face interaction, networking, etc.) we will also investigate the "Actors," "Typology," "Accessibility," "Social Displacement," and "Entrepreneurial Character" (See Table 1). The data for our model were collected through document analysis (Education City land use plan, Qatar Foundation advertising material, etc.) and on-site, fieldwork observations carried out in Doha from February to May 2013. To facilitate comparisons, an additional column referring to the current literature (Yigitcanlar et al., 2008; den Heijer et al., 2012; König, 2013) on popular knowledge developments in countries such as Taiwan, Finland, Singapore, the Netherlands, and Canada has been provided. Finally, for the sake of clarity, we will use the

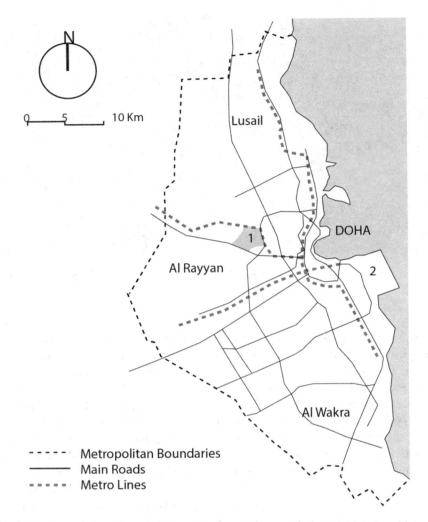

Figure 4. Doha Metropolitan Area: (1) Education City; (2) airport. *Source*: author's own elaboration

existing term *Knowledge Precincts (KPs)* (Yigitcanlar et al., 2007) when referring to knowledge developments in the global North while the term *Knowledge Megaprojects (KMs)*, which better connects to and complements urban studies literature in Asia (Shatkin, 2008; Elsheshtawy, 2010; Rizzo, 2014; Koch, 2014), will be used to refer to the Gulf case and by extension to the global South.

Results

When compared to literature on KPs in the North, the first major divergent aspect is that Education City is primarily a public project, i.e., financed by the central government through its Qatar Foundation, rather than being a city-level initiative (see the "Client" theme in Table 1). When discussing Dutch case studies, den Heijer and others (2012: 107) stress the importance of city/higher education collaboration as a factor of "great importance in stimulating the knowledge economy." Therefore, the "entrepreneurial

Table 1. Comparison of Education City with literature on Knowledge Precincts (KPs) in the West

Themes	Education City	KPs
Actor(s)	Qatar Foundation (government)	Multi-level: university, development corporations, city/municipality, region/state
Entrepreneurial Character	Low/none; it is government funded	High; it is the result of some form of public and private partnership (PPP)
Type of Development	Megaproject	Incremental, urban regeneration/redevelopment
Branding	"Putting the country on the map" (nation-wide strategy)	Emerging knowledge city (city-level strategy)
Land Use Model	Large, single-zones	Compact, mixed-use
Social Connectivity	Low: public spaces are too large to generate density of interactions	High: increased chances for face-to-face interaction
Learning and Experimental Values	Higher Education is the main theme	Integration between learning and research
Centrality	New development area outside the city center	Regeneration of the existing urban areas
Accessibility	Gated—accessible to knowledge workers	Open to and integrated with the city
Social Displacement	Temporary racialized workers building facilities for future knowledge inhabitants	Gentrification can be an outcome of urban regeneration/redevelopment

character" of Education City, i.e., the level of private-public finance synergies to implement the project, is second to none. This is in line with other megaprojects in the region that aim primarily at strengthening the leadership of the ruling family and in so doing can be considered more political projects (Ponzini, 2011; Crot, 2013; Rizzo, 2016). As a result, Education City is implemented all at once, as a one-off development, in contrast to the incremental implementation of KPs ("Type of Development"). Moreover, Education City is deployed as a brand to visualize the country, Qatar, to the global audiences portraying the campus as the initiative "personifying national progress" (from QF advertising material) and contributing to "unlocking human potential" (this latter quote being the slogan of Qatar Foundation). In the KPs reviewed in the literature, branding occurs at the city scale, to boost its competitive edge against other rising or established knowledge centers. For example, in the case of 22@bcn design is deployed to symbolize the transition of "industrial of 22a Poblenou [and thus of the whole of Barcelona] to the knowledge-based 22@" (Yigitcanlar et al., 2008).

Furthermore, Education City campus is a gated community with single-zone planning (see "Land Use model"), thus allowing little possibility for walking and encounters. Compact and city-like (dense and integrated) developments are major characteristics of KPs in the West since, Yigitcanlar and others (2007) argue, they foster a greater degree of social interaction between the knowledge inhabitants (see "Social Connectivity"). In KPs in countries such as Australia and Luxembourg, compactness and density play a crucial role in fostering innovation and creative thinking ("Learning and Experimental Values"). A dense and complex urban setting is thought to create the conditions for a better integration of learning, research, and development (the triple helix model) and thus is a main strategy to foster economic growth and innovation both in the Dutch cases discussed by den Heijer and others (2012) and the university campuses in Gothenburg and Luxembourg studied by König and Evans (2013). On the other hand, Education City is a low-density, sprawled campus where signature buildings randomly dot a huge expanse of outdoor space that is impossible to cross during the hot summer period (i.e., from April to October)—or even inappropriate given the local customs (e.g., clothing, privacy, etc.). Thus, there is no chance for random encounters and/or knowledge exchange within the Qatari campus.

Moreover, in KBUD literature "Centrality" is an important aspect, and KPs are often located in existing urban areas that are in need of densification or regeneration strategies—see the case of the new campus of Luxembourg University located in the industrial district of Belval (König, 2013). The integration between KPs and the existing city is thought to be crucial for the final success of the enterprise (Yigitcanlar et al., 2008). In the case of Education City and many other mega-developments in the Gulf, KMs tend to be located outside the existing city, in areas that were either undeveloped (desertic) or with low levels of urbanization—thus, easy to be redeveloped but involving long commuting times. One more crucial aspect to set Education City apart from KPs in the West is "Accessibility" since access to this mega-gated knowledge community is permitted to employees, students, and knowledge workers only. This aspect has a major impact on the social geography of the campus which sees the overrepresentation of wealthy, knowledge inhabitants in command positions over racialized workers (typically coming from South Asia, and Africa—see Nagy, 2006) who are often employed in building construction or maintenance jobs. If we look at this from the perspective of "Social Displacement," we can see that while in Education City social displacement (either of the former residents, or the temporary, racialized working community) is a precondition to implementing the project (Rizzo, 2013), in KPs in the West (see the case of 22@bcn in Barcelona: König, 2013) social displacement is the more the secondary, but still very important, result of infrastructure upgrading and rising real estate values (i.e., gentrification).

Conclusions: Will Knowledge Megaprojects Transform the Gulf's Economies?

In this paper, we have analyzed the emerging phenomenon of Knowledge Megaprojects (KMs) in the Gulf region. KMs are the spatial outcomes of a number of ongoing trends in the Gulf and other Asian countries such as the push for economic diversification away from natural resources, aspirations of the governments and local elites to become knowledge hubs, the internationalization of higher education and the IBC phenomenon, the increased mobility of knowledge workers, and the increasing competition between cities to attract knowledge inhabitants (workers, students, etc.). By building upon the experience of consumption megaprojects in the region and other Asian emerging markets (most notably Singapore), KMs in the Gulf aim to deliver a self-contained, public funded, one-off development that in many cases had very little to do with the existing city.

When we look at our case study, Education City, we can suggest that while it resembles similar KPs found in the West, it strongly differs from these in a number of ways. While KPs in the West are far from perfect (e.g., considering issues such as gentrification, entrepreneurialism, commodification, etc.), the case of Education City highlights a number of critical issues such as top-down policy (to strengthen the current leadership), social displacements (the use of racialized transnational workers to build the campuses), and an unsustainable land-use model (a mega gated community that, given the local climate, does not encourage walking) which are likely to hinder a smooth transition to a post-oil economy. The Education City gated campus is very similar to those described by Graham and Marvin (2001) in their "Splintering Metropolis:" the KM while aiming at reaching out to the international knowledge community (also thanks to its numerous IBCs), is disconnected (since it is gated, its accesses are controlled day and night by security, and developed in an area far from the urbanized core) from the surrounding city. The wall that fences the campus off the surrounding city is a physical and symbolic barrier to city integration (Jackson and Della Dora, 2009; Ouis, 2011). The lack of interest in better integration between the existing city and the campus is strengthened by the different architectural language deployed by the campus' architects; while outside Education City urbanization is anonymous and cheap, within the campus it is spectacular, technologically advanced, and the scale is monumental. We have seen that this exclusive character is not conducive to fostering "Social Connectivity" and "Learning and Experimental Values," two aspects suggested by Yigitcanlar and others (2008) as crucial for attracting knowledge workers and driving innovation. Also the process behind the implementation of Education City is characterized by a number of issues: the rationale for the KM is more to strengthen national leadership than to drive change and build capacity in Doha (Rizzo, 2016); the megaproject is presented as the brainchild of the leader and it isn't built upon a robust dialogue with local stakeholders; the implementation of Education City is extremely violent as it entailed the full removal of the previous tissue and the deployment of exploited, racialized workers.

We argue that Education City replicates rather than heals the current segregated development pattern in Doha—this latter being the result of oil wealth. Education City, rather than being an innovative urban type, is built after old land-use formulas whereby "tabula rasa" planning, gated development, and car-based transport is preferred to urban regeneration, participatory planning, and compact neighborhoods (Yigitcanlar et al., 2008; den Heijer et al., 2012; König, 2013). In its current form, Education City is bound to fail in transforming Qatar into a mature knowledge economy. From a planning point of view, there are alternatives that would lead to more innovative, just, and environmentally sustainable knowledge developments that would be integrated into the existing city. First, local urban planning authorities should create the conditions for urban regeneration of the existing centers with knowledge functions: this would foster integration and accessibility while ensuring lower costs for infrastructures and less car-based commuting. Second, knowledge developments should work as test-beds for more compact development that is also climate-sensitive (thus encouraging walking and social connection). Third, the decision-making process should be opened up to the public and the local knowledge community (which is often excluded by decision-makers). Along these lines, we see a great opportunity for the local academy, especially for the local architecture and planning programs, to make crucial and critical (rather than passive and celebrative) contributions towards a just and sustainable transition to the post-carbon economy of the Gulf.

Note

1. Until three years ago, in Doha's The Pearl it was possible to consume alcohol in restaurants opened to the public unlike in the existing city where alcohol consumption is permitted only within hotels and private, indoor premises. However, this exemption was then amended in 2012 when local Qataris complained to the authorities. In Dubai's Palm Jumeirah, alcohol is still served in a number of activities.

Disclosure Statement

No potential conflict of interest was reported by the author.

ORCID

Agatino Rizzo http://orcid.org/0000-0001-6831-8857

Bibliography

K. Adham, "Rediscovering the Island: Doha's Urbanity from Pearls to Spectacle," in Y. Elsheshtawy, ed., *The Evolving Arab City: Tradition, Modernity and Urban Development* (Abingdon: Routledge, 2008) 218–256.

F. Al Buainain, *Urbanisation in Qatar: A Study of the Residential and Commercial Land Development in Doha City, 1970-1997* (Salford, UK: University of Salford, PhD Thesis, 1999).

P. G. Altbach and J. Knight, "The Internationalization of Higher Education: Motivations and Realities," *Journal of Studies in International Education* 11: 3–4(2007) 290–305.

S. Bagaeen, "Brand Dubai: The Instant City; or the Instantly Recognizable City," *International Planning Studies* 12: 2 (2007) 173–197.

Y. Cao, "Branch Campuses in Asia and the Pacific: Definitions, Challenges and Strategies," *Comparative & International Higher Education* 3 (2011) 8–10.

M. Castells, *The Rise of the Network Society: The Information age: Economy, Society and Culture* (Massachusetts and Oxford: Blackwell, 1996).

M. Castells, and P. Hall, *Technopoles of the World: The Making of Twenty-First-Century Industrial Complexes* (London: Routledge, 1994).

D. Charles, "The Role of Universities in Building Knowledge Cities in Australia," *Built Environment* 37: 3 (2011) 281–298.

J.W. Creswell, *Research Design: Qualitative, Quantitative, and Mixed Methods Approaches* (Thousand Oaks: Sage, 2009).

Cross-Border Education Research Team (C-BERT), *C-BERT Branch Campus Listing* <http://globalhighered.org/branchcampuses.php> Accessed January 30, 2015.

L. Crot, "Planning for Sustainability in Non-democratic Polities: The Case of Masdar City," *Urban Studies* 50: 13 (2013) 2809–2825.

F. Cugurullo, "Urban Eco-Modernisation and the Policy Context of New Eco-City Projects: Where Masdar City Fails And Why," *Urban Studies* 53: 11 (2016) 2417–2433.

A. Datta, and A. Shaban, eds., *Mega-Urbanization in the Global South: Fast Cities and New Urban Utopias of the Postcolonial State* (London: Routledge, 2017).

C. Davidson, "Abu Dhabi's New Economy: Oil, Investment and Domestic Development," *Middle East Policy* 16: 2 (2009) 59–79.

Y. Elsheshtawy, *Dubai: Behind an Urban Spectacle* (London: Routledge, 2010).

M.C. Ewers, and E.J. Malecki, "Leapfrogging Into the Knowledge Economy: Assessing the Economic Development Strategies of the Arab Gulf States," *Tijdschrift voor economische en sociale geografie* 101: 5 (2010) 494–508.

(GAD) General Secretariat of the Executive Council, Abu Dhabi Council for Economic Development, *The Abu Dhabi Economic Vision 2030* (Abu Dhabi: Department of Planning and Economy, 2008).

P.K. Gellert, and B.D. Lynch, "Mega-projects as Displacements," *International Social Science Journal* 55: 175 (2003) 15–25.

S. Graham, and S. Marvin, *Splintering Urbanism, Networked Infrastructures, Technological Mobilities and the Urban Condition* (London: Routledge, 2001).

(GSDP) General Secretariat for Development Planning, *Qatar National Vision 2030* (Doha: General Secretariat for Development Planning, 2008).

A. den Heijer, J. de Vries, and H. de Jonge, "5. Developing Knowledge Cities: Towards Aligning Urban and Campus Strategies," in M. Van Geenhuizen, and P. Nijkamp, eds., *Creative Knowledge Cities: Myths, Visions and Realities* (Northampton: Edward Elgar Publishing, 2012) 104–131.

M. Jackson, and V. della Dora, "'Dreams So Big Only the Sea Can Hold Them': Man-Made Islands as Anxious Spaces, Cultural Icons, and Travelling Visions," *Environment and planning A* 41: 9 (2009) 2086–2104.

R.V. Knight, "Knowledge-Based Development: Policy and Planning Implications for Cities," *Urban Studies* 32: 2 (1995) 225–260.

N. Koch, "'Building Glass Refrigerators in the Desert': Discourses of Urban Sustainability and Nation Building in Qatar," *Urban Geography* 35: 8 (2014) 1118–1139.

A. König, ed., *Regenerative Sustainable Development of Universities and Cities: the Role of Living Laboratories* (Northampton: Edward Elgar Publishing, 2013).

A. König, and J. Evans, "Introduction: Experimenting for Sustainable Development? Living Laboratories, Social Learning and the Role of the university," in A. König, ed., *Regenerative Sustainable Development of Universities and Cities: the Role of Living Laboratories* (Northampton: Edward Elgar Publishing, 2013) 1–23.

R. Mohammad, J. D. Sidaway, "Shards and Stages: Migrant Lives, Power, and Space Viewed from Doha, Qatar," *Annals of the American Association of Geographers* 106: 6(2016), 1397–1417.

S. Moser, M. Swain, and M.H. Alkhabbaz, "King Abdullah Economic City: Engineering Saudi Arabia's post-oil future," *Cities* 45 (2015) 71–80.

S. Nagy, "This Time I Think I'll Try a Filipina': Global and Local Influences on Relations between Foreign Household Workers and Their Employers in Doha, Qatar," *City & Society* 10: 1(1998) 83–103.

S. Nagy, "Making Room for Migrants, Making Sense of Difference: Spatial and Ideological Expressions of Social Diversity in Urban Qatar," *Urban Studies* 43: 1(2006) 119–137.

National Science Foundation (NSF), *Science and Engineering Indicators* <http://www.nsf.gov/statistics/seind10/c6/c6s1.htm> Accessed January 30, 2015.

P. Ouis, "'And an Island Never Cries': Cultural and Societal Perspectives on the Mega Development of Islands in the United Arab Emirates," in V. Badescu, and R.B. Cathcart, *Macro-engineering Seawater in Unique Environments: arid Lowlands and Water Bodies Rehabilitation* (Berlin: Springer Berlin Heidelberg, 2011) 59–75.

J.E. Peterson, "Life After Oil: Economic Alternatives for the Arab Gulf States," *Mediterranean Quarterly* 20: 3 (2009) 1–18.

D. Ponzini, "Large Scale Development Projects and Star Architecture in the Absence of Democratic Politics: The Case of Abu Dhabi, UAE," *Cities* 28 (2011) 251–259.

M. Riad, "Some Aspects of Petro-Urbanism in the Arab Gulf States," *Bulletin of the Faculty of Humanities and Social Sciences (Qatar University)* 4 (1981) 7–24.

A. Rizzo, "Metro Doha," *Cities* 31 (2013) 533–543.

A. Rizzo, "Rapid Urban Development and National Master Planning in Arab Gulf Countries. Qatar as a Case Study," *Cities* 39 (2014) 50–57.

A. Rizzo, "Sustainable Urban Development and Green Megaprojects in the Arab States of the Gulf Region: Limitations, Covert Aims, and Unintended Outcomes in Doha, Qatar," *International Planning Studies* 22 (2016) 1–14.

A. Rizzo, "From Petro-Urbanism to Knowledge Megaprojects in the Persian Gulf: Qatar Foundation's Education City," in A. Datta, and A. Shaban, eds., *Mega-Urbanization in the Global South: Fast Cities and New Urban Utopias of the Postcolonial State* (London: Routledge, 2017) 101–122.

G.D. Shank, *Qualitative Research: A Personal Skills Approach* (Upper Saddle River: Pearson Merrill Prentice Hall, 2006).

G. Shatkin, "The City and the Bottom Line: Urban Megaprojects and the Privatization of Planning in Southeast Asia," *Environment and Planning A* 40: 2 (2008) 383–401.

Webometrics, *Ranking Web of Universities* <www.webometrics.info> Accessed January 30, 2015.

S. Wilkins, M.S. Balakrishnan, and J. Huisman, "Student Choice in Higher Education: Motivations for Choosing to Study at an International Branch Campus," *Journal of Studies in International Education* 16: 5 (2012) 413–433.

T. Yigitcanlar, S. Baum, and S. Horton, "Attracting and Retaining Knowledge Workers in Knowledge Cities," *Journal of Knowledge Management* 11: 5 (2007) 6–17.

T. Yigitcanlar, K. Velibeyoglu, and C. Martinez-Fernandez, "Rising Knowledge Cities: the Role of Urban Knowledge Precincts," *Journal of Knowledge Management* 12: 5 (2008) 8–20.

Catch Me if You Can: Workplace Mobility and Big Data

Filipa Pajević and Richard G. Shearmur

ABSTRACT
A growing number of workers, particularly in the knowledge and service sectors, can perform their work at multiple locations, and it is decreasingly realistic to assume, as researchers and planners have traditionally done, that employment in cities occurs in fixed locations. This suggests that census data or establishment registries do not fully capture where economic activity takes place. Given the role that ICTs play in enabling daytime workplace mobility, and given that they generate substantial amounts of real-time, geolocated data, we ask whether these Big Data can shed light upon the trajectories of mobile workers at the urban scale.

Introduction

The proliferation of smart devices and other workplace technologies has not only made work more flexible, but also highly mobile. Indeed, people—often those in intellectual and service-oriented jobs (Kesselring, 2006), or "creative work" (Florida, 2010)—are increasingly able to work from a variety of locations (Brown and O'Hara, 2003; Hislop and Axtell, 2007, 2009), arrange meetings and meeting places in real time, and it is less and less realistic to suppose, as researchers have traditionally done (e.g., Shearmur et al., 2007) that they have a fixed place of work, i.e., the office (see also Felstead et al., 2005). While not all workers can (or want to) take advantage of these possibilities, an increasing number do (Kesselring, 2015; Loacker and Śliwa, 2015). We define this phenomenon as *workplace mobility*, or the ability of workers to carry out work-related activities at any time and at any place as a result of the increasing flexibility of work and work policies, advancements in workplace technology, and temporality of contracts.

This workplace mobility can occur at a variety of spatial and time scales. During the course of the day, work can take place from an array of locations (vehicles, third spaces, parks, home, office ...), but the possibilities afforded by computerization of work-related activities also enhance the capacity to perform work during business trips (in hotels, lobbies, airports) and while traveling for leisure—the temporalities of which may be weekly, monthly, annually or irregularly. From an abstract perspective, Häger-strand's (1982) space-time prism—representing the spatial extent of activity given space-time constraints (often associated with the need to be at a specific workplace at specific times)—needs to be rethought in the light of work's decreasing spatial fixity.

However, before addressing this wider question, the more straightforward one of where work actually takes place needs to be addressed. Traditional approaches to the study of employment location—using census data or establishment registries that assume a fixed place of work—no longer fully capture where economic activity actually takes place and where economic value is created. This is not only of academic interest, but of practical importance to planning and design: as public spaces, transport infrastructure and places of entertainment (such as restaurants and cafés) become places of work and value creation, so the way these places are thought of and are incorporated into strategic economic thinking at the city level needs to evolve. Likewise, the role traditionally assigned to clusters, employment centers, and business parks (often assumed to foster interactions by virtue of the co-location of workers) will need to be reassessed in the light of these new behaviors (See Martin and Sunley, 2003; Torre, 2008; Shearmur, 2011; Huber, 2012).

Given the role that information and communication technologies (ICT) play in enabling workplace mobility, and given that ICTs generate huge amounts of real time, geo-located data—phone users can be tracked, the intensity of data and line use can be geolocated and recorded throughout the day (See Calabrese et al., 2007; Reades et al., 2009; Tranos and Nijkamp, 2015), Twitter posts can reveal activities taking place at a particular place and time, etc. (See Shelton et al., 2015)—in this paper we explore whether these Big Data can—in principle at least—shed light upon the trajectories of knowledge and service workers at the urban scale. Given that traditional approaches to the study of employment location are not capable of capturing these trajectories, to what extent can Big Data be incorporated into research design and methodology? Can the technologies that enable workplace mobility be used to extract data on where work is being performed in cities?

The current discussion of Big Data has tended to be of two types: it has either been data-driven, providing examples of its use (e.g., Mayer-Schönberger and Cukier, 2013; Feinlieb, 2014), or it has been epistemological (and sometimes political), describing the nature, limitations, and possible dangers of Big Data in a general way (e.g., Kitchin, 2013, 2014). In this paper we briefly review this literature, looking at some applications of Big Data in recent social scientific research (mainly in urban studies), as well as some of the discourses on the opportunities and challenges of Big Data, in order to understand the extent to which we could rely on them to reveal the spatial underpinnings of knowledge and service work.

What are Big Data? On the one hand, Big Data are information: they are usually derived from users of a particular technology or from sensors, without people being aware of the data collection (Nunan and di Domenico, 2013). Their usefulness derives from their volume (Delort, 2015), velocity, and variety (Kitchin, 2013). The metadata, not the content, are often the value of Big Data. They typically do not reveal the nature of a event, but when, how, and where an event occurs (Lyon, 2014). On the other hand, Big Data are a tool: the rapid rate at which they are refreshed, enable them to be used in feedback loops, altering behavior (or at least the networks that underpin the behavior) in almost real time (Eagle and Greene, 2014; Feinlieb, 2014). Although data have always had this dual aspect—observation of a phenomenon and input for action—the speed and scale at which this can now be done are leading to qualitative changes in the feedback mechanism: from being a fairly slow, deliberative process, open to analysis and debate, it is becoming a real-time phenomenon guided by algorithms that are often opaque (Finn, 2017).

The opaque nature of Big Data algorithms, and of the underlying data themselves, is due to their operational, and often private, nature (Helbing, 2015). These data are not gathered by statistical agencies or through surveys, which focus on a pre-conceptualized population, on precise variable definitions, and for which adequate sampling is important. They are usually gathered opportunistically from users of particular networks or technologies: the data are massive, can be used to influence (and, hopefully, improve) the particular function for which they are gathered, but their usefulness in a social scientific context, to further understanding of social and economic processes that are multidimensional and that extend beyond users of particular technologies remains open to question (Mahrt and Scharkow, 2013; Lyon, 2014; Kitchin and McArdle, 2016; van Meeteren and Poorthuis, 2017).

Although Big Data have already become mainstream in urban studies (e.g., Batty, 2013; Rathore et al., 2016), with researchers using social media platforms such as Twitter and Flickr to understand gentrification and urban density (Hwang and Sampson, 2014), and web-based service platforms such as Über to understand the impact of these mobility services on traffic congestion (Hall and Krueger, 2015), it is difficult to determine whether the new wave of Big Data analysis is producing valuable insight and not merely vignettes of urban complexity. We argue that in spite of their potential, Big Data encounter difficulty when multidimensional information is required, particularly relating to emerging phenomena that require exploration: while tracking the whereabouts of people in real time is now relatively straightforward, understanding the *why* and the *wherefore* is far more difficult.

This article has two aims: first, to explain why our current knowledge about where work is actually performed in cities is increasingly imprecise; and second, to discuss whether research designs and methods used to study the location of economic activity can usefully integrate Big Data in order to capture the new (and mobile) geography of work.

Changes in Work and the Workplace: The Challenge of Locating Where Value-Creation Occurs

It is not possible to review all the changes that have occurred in the workplace and in the nature of work since the early 1990s. Two key changes will briefly be described. First, the types of contract and employment experience which current workforce entrants face differ from those that prevailed prior to the 1990s. Temporary contracts allow workers to engage in multiple activities throughout their careers, either as independent contractors (or freelancers), or as full-time employees whose work entails movement across sectors and between projects. At present, industrial and organizational behavior scholarship is focused on understanding whether such contractual arrangements make workers vulnerable or provide a sense of empowerment (e.g., Cook, 2015; Warner, 2015). Little attention is paid to the geography of employment based on temporary, multiple, and/or flexible contracts.

Second, for many types of work—particularly those types that are deemed "creative" (Florida, 2010) and that of "symbolic analysts" (Reich, 1992)—technology allows value creation to occur from a wide variety of locations (Schieman and Young, 2010; Kesselring, 2015): the assumption is that for these kinds of jobs, the nature of the workplace is changing. A more exact approximation of the kinds of jobs that are most subjected to such changes remains, to our knowledge, elusive. Current definitions are either too broad, or focus on one specific industry or sector. A more complete overview and conceptualization of mobile work have yet to emerge in the literature. Nonetheless, both of these changes—the temporality of contractual arrangements and multi-location work—are connected, and both should lead to a reappraisal of the idea of "place-of-work."

Prior to the 1990s, most young people entering the workforce, in particular if they were graduates, could entertain reasonable expectations of full-time employment, and of a career structured by periodic moves between different stable jobs (Krahn and Lowe, 1998). A quarter of a century later, young people are entering an economy in which flexibility of work is commonplace in the app-based on-demand/gig economy. As Boltanski and Chiapello (2005) presciently describe in the case of France, and as Sennett (1999) also observed, work is increasingly project based, people are integrated and dropped from projects on the basis of their specific skills, and each person is continuously monitoring their surroundings for the next project on which to work. Only a small number of more senior managers, themselves often involved in a variety of projects, benefit from stability, but this stability often reflects their relationships and position within professional networks rather than stable salaried employment. As Friedman (2014) argues with respect to the United States, echoing Capelli and Keller (2013):

> A growing number of American workers are no longer employed in "jobs" with a long-term connection with a company but are hired for "gigs" under "flexible" arrangements as "independent contractors" or "consultants," working only to complete a particular task or for defined time and with no more connection with their employer than there might be between a consumer and a particular brand of soap or potato chips. (Friedman, 2014: 171)

This type of job has been growing particularly rapidly in the construction, business service, and other services sectors, but growth has been fast across the whole economy: about 85 percent of all new jobs created between 2005 and 2013 in the US economy had alternative contractual arrangements (i.e., alternative to contracts "with fixed hours, location and certain expectations of security")—up from only 3 percent between 1995 and 2001, and 55 percent between 2001 and 2005 (Friedman, 2014: 176). From a spatial perspective, Kesselring (2015: 572) cites a German study that found that "in 2008, 37 percent of the interviewees... were working to a various extent from changing locations," though he recognizes the paucity of studies recording where work actually takes place.

The second factor—linked to, but distinct from, the increasing flexibility of work—is the revolution in information and communication technologies that began in the 1970s and 1980s with the slow development and introduction of the Internet and of cellphones, which took off from the mid-1990s as these technologies became ubiquitous, reliable, and increasingly mobile. This has had a variety of consequences. The first is that many alternatives to the traditional workplace have become feasible, such as trains (Lyons et al., 2013) and cars (Hislop, 2013). At first, the principal alternative that was envisaged was working from home. As we saw above, our understanding of where economic activity occurs is premised on the notion of "place-of-work." From the 1990s, the Internet and ICTs made it increasingly feasible for employees and self-employed people to operate, at least part of the time, from home (see teleworking literature, e.g., Nilles, 1994; Handy and Mokhtarian, 1995). While these studies acknowledge some of the impacts of new communications technologies, they retain the idea that specific activities occur in specific places—in this case work occurs either at home or in the office. Kwan's (2002) discussion of the changing space-time matrices of everyday life is also premised on access to the Internet at fixed locations.

However, it is the advent of mobile phones and other handheld devices that has more fundamentally altered spatial work patterns (Katz and Aakhus, 2002; Licoppe, 2004). Most basically, these devices allow access to social media, to web-based documents, to conference calls, from almost any urban location. More subtly, they allow for the real-time coordination of meetings and of other activities. And these two changes are having major impact on work location, particularly for younger people who are more attuned to and at ease with these possibilities than older workers (Deal et al, 2010; Rainie and Wellman, 2012).

Indeed, with ubiquitous access to tools and information required for knowledge work (a broad term that encompasses creative and symbolic work), the assumption that knowledge workers need to be present at the office as they perform work becomes questionable. Some firms appear to have redefined the purpose of having a fixed place of work, treating the workplace as an arena for social and business encounters, it being understood that when a particular task requires concentration one retreats to a café, a park, or to one's home (Bennett et al., 2010; Waber et al., 2014). Furthermore, transport networks themselves have become places where work occurs: what Augé (1995) characterized as non-spaces—platforms, sidewalks, rails, airports—have now become places from which people phone, respond to e-mails, arrange meetings, write; in short, places from which economic activity can be, and often is, performed. A study of business travelers and their car journeys revealed that they perform much of their work on the road (Lyons and Urry, 2004), changing how we understand productivity and evaluate the importance of travel time in the Information Age.

That said, people and economic activity are necessarily situated, and people necessarily take part in face-to-face interactions. Thus, even if the permanent co-location of workers is no longer as important (Bathelt and Turi, 2011; Glucker, 2011), space continues to have a role as support for meetings, and also as support for transport networks that enable the mobility of agents attending these meetings (Agrawal et al., 2006). To use Castells' (2011) terminology, physical space undergirds not only the nodes, but also the flows, of a networked society. The way in which this undergirding occurs, and the functions that take place along networks or at meeting places require exploration, since physical networks and physical meeting places need to be designed, built, and maintained.

While Castells' (2011) ideas refer to global and national urban systems, they are also relevant in forming preliminary ideas about intra-urban work location—especially concerning worker mobility. Indeed, one of the limitations of current research on employment location is that it focuses on where firms locate (Parr, 2002; Meijers, 2007; Currid, 2007; Shearmur, 2012). However, firm location may only be the *official* place of work, and not the *actual* place of work. Consider, for instance, business consultants who often perform their work at their clients' location (see Hislop and Axtell, 2009).

What is more, literature that emphasizes the benefits of geographic clusters assumes that most workers actually perform their work in—or very close to—their official place-of-work. However, there are growing reasons to question this assumption. The first reason to question the idea that economy-related interactions occur within localized clusters is the fact that such local effects are not always observed where expected (in high-tech business parks or in Central Business Districts, for instance): indeed, when they have been sought in a systematic way (Massey et al., 1992; Suarez-Villa and Walrod, 1997; Gordon and McCann, 2000; Huber, 2012; Shearmur, 2012) the results have often been inconclusive at best. These studies reveal that there is no reason to believe that work-related interactions are localized—interaction within London's finance sector being one of the exceptions (Gordon and McCann, 2000).

Meanwhile, in literature on worker mobility, geography comes second to the psychological (individual and collective) effects of mobile work (See Cooper et al. 2002; Brown and O'Hara, 2003; Felstead et al., 2005; Halford, 2005; Lassen, 2009; Kesselring, 2015). Studies that do focus on the geography of mobile work are few and confirm that work is increasingly occurring away from the office, but still focus on working at home while ignoring—largely because of lack of data—work performed in other types of urban spaces (see Felstead, 2012).

The two key changes described—the increasing flexibility of work, and advancements in ICT—call for a re-evaluation of the "place-of-work." The proliferation of temporary contracts, the multiplicity of projects undertaken by a single employee, and the multi-location of work are some of the key characteristics of increasing flexibility of work. Workers often alternate between projects, or line up engagements that require them to be accessible and perform work beyond office hours, producing a work–life balance that is less about balancing and more about the blurring of work–life time and space (Demerouti et al., 2014).

Given these considerations, we suggest that work should be conceptualized as taking place along geographic trajectories (Massey, 2005) punctuated by moments of fixity. In order to verify this hypothesis, the nature of work needs to be considered (is all work equally mobile?) and means to test it devised. We first consider work, and then consider Big Data derived from ICTs as a possible means to verify the hypothesis.

A Typology of Worker Mobility

Workplace mobility is clearly a growing phenomenon. Management scholars argue that "mobility for work" has become a key feature of professional life. Looking at the trajectories of academics and theatrical artists, Loacker and Śliwa (2015) conclude that mobility at a variety of temporal and spatial scales is necessary to maintain economic and professional status.

We have so far suggested that workplace mobility principally affects knowledge-related work: however, the reality is more complex and nuanced. To capture some of this nuance, we have drawn out six dimensions of workplace mobility, based upon the work done by mobilities scholars (e.g., Kesselring, 2006; Urry, 2007; Baerenholdt, 2013), management and organization studies (Taylor and Spicer, 2007; Borg and Söderlund, 2013), and our own understanding of the phenomenon:

- *Meetings and face-to-face interactions*: even the most mobile of jobs require times and places at which face-to-face meetings occur (with clients, students, co-workers). Mobile technology can help coordinate these meetings, but often it is more expedient to have pre-arranged meeting times—for instance weekly team meetings or times at which a lecture is given. Furthermore, for some jobs meeting face-to-face with the client is necessary for a successful working relationship: these meetings are regular and often take place at the clients' locations (see Hislop and Axtell, 2009).

- *Mobility as freedom/choice or as a constraint/necessity:* for example, new academics and researchers tend to exhibit higher levels of mobility as they seek to gain experience and employment—for them mobility is a necessity, while established academics move seldom and move by choice (Loacker and Śliwa, 2015).
- *Status and mobility:* spatial mobility can be associated with upward or downward shifts in mobility (see Sheller and Urry, 2006), but given that the experience of mobility can be different for different types of workers (choice or necessity) there is no automatic connection between status and mobility. Indeed, workers engaged in home cleaning, dog walking, and personal care are mobile, and increasingly coordinate their timetables by way of mobile communications, yet do not benefit from the high status often associated with knowledge workers. Within this latter category, young workers engaged in "gig" work do not themselves benefit from particularly high status.
- *Fixed versus unconstrained mobility:* some mobile jobs are closely tied to networks. For example, high-status airline pilots, as well as lower status truck drivers, perform their economic activity while moving, but their activity is closely connected with heavy equipment (airplanes, trucks) and with particular routes along networks (air routes, highways). In opposition to this type of fixed mobility, unconstrained mobility corresponds to knowledge workers who can perform their job from any location that has a phone or a Wi-Fi connection.
- *Potential versus actual workplace mobility:* it is not because workplace mobility is possible that it is actually performed: recently Marissa Mayer, the director of Yahoo! "order [ed] workers back to the office" (Miller and Rampell, 2013). This reveals two things: first that workday mobility is a reality, and, second, that while it is enabled by technology it is only implemented if the work environment and culture accepts it.
- *Not all jobs have potential for mobility:* finally, many jobs remain immobile out of necessity. Factory work, and other work closely associated with immobile capital equipment, can only occur in a fixed location. Likewise, many service jobs—from restaurant service to hotel management—require presence on a particular site, and interactions with clients at particular places.

Economic activity has not been thought about in this way before: mobility has been studied in terms of commuting, business travel, and—increasingly—of specific locations (e.g., third places or hybrid spaces) and networks (e.g., railway networks) where it can occur: but jobs themselves, and the creation of economic value, still tends to be associated with a "place-of-work."

Faced with this new way of conceptualizing place-of-work (which remains hypothetical despite its plausibility), and in the light of our previous research on metropolitan structures and job location (that has relied on census data and establishment surveys, e.g., Shearmur et al., 2007; Shearmur, 2012), to what extent can Big Data further our exploration and understanding of these new trends? This is a particular instance of a wider question: notwithstanding the quantity and sophistication of data now available, can their analysis help us understand new (and hence poorly conceptualized and understood) social and economic processes, even in cases such as this where the new process is closely tied to ICT and is fundamentally one of geolocation?

Having discussed in some detail the reasons for re-conceptualizing the location of work activity, and after highlighting the way in which it is enabled by ICTs, it is to this wider question that we now turn.

Big Data and Urban Studies

In the previous sections, we argued that economic activity and value creation can no longer be associated in a straightforward way with a "place-of-work." This has always been an approximation (there have always been traveling salesmen and taxi drivers, for example), but an approximation that has guided the way city managers and planners think about cities—with areas zoned for economic activity, buildings assigned specific uses, and specific neighborhoods and clusters understood as being the locus of economic activity. It is increasingly important to envisage new ways of apprehending the urban space-economy, of identifying how economic activity draws upon urban spaces and unfolds across them. In this section we consider whether Big Data, specifically those derived from cellphones and social networking sites, can be used for this purpose.

Indeed, the communication and transport networks that support daily mobility are themselves generating vast amounts of passive data (Mayer-Schönberger and Cukier, 2013). There is considerable interest and optimism in the possibility that this information can be transformed into knowledge that could be applied to problem solving (Miller, 2010). Given the size of these data, and their rather disparate nature, data mining techniques are often envisaged that could lead to new knowledge (or at least to uncovering unsuspected relationships that require understanding and theorization). Furthermore, many of these data are associated with location coordinates or zones: this is seen as a tremendous opportunity for spatial sciences. Telecommunication patterns are now being used for real-time urban analysis (Steenbruggen et al., 2015), e-ticketing can provide new information on commuting patterns (Batty, 2009; 2013), and participatory GIS and social networks can offer insights into new uses of space and neighborhood dynamics (Shelton et al., 2015). Some even claim that we are now in the position to see, perhaps for the first time, the mechanics of the global economy as well as to better understand society (including the city and its functions) (Tranos and Nijkamp, 2013).

Notwithstanding the usefulness of Big Data for immediate response to issues such as traffic and crowd management, it is difficult to assess the extent to which Big Data enable understanding (as opposed to tracking and real-time optimization) of the underlying layers of the global economy and the generation of knowledge on changes in our society and cities. It is one thing to track cellphones, follow vehicles, or assess flows—it is quite another to understand what is occurring and what people are doing. In particular, it is difficult to assess whether an activity (being at point "A," driving from "A" to "B") is being performed for economic, leisure, personal or family motives. Yet to understand the interaction between work, location, and trajectories through the city, that is what would be required.

Much of Big Data's power lies in its combination of volume and diversity. However, without information on the population being observed, and without the capacity to cross-reference much of the information obtained (e.g., we may know where a cellphone is, but who is using it and why?) insights are generated by way of inference and correlations. In many ways Big Data, well suited to identifying recent historic trends, are poorly adapted to uncovering change. It would require careful matching of new and existing data types for them to generate more concrete knowledge on the changing urban dynamic (Becker et al., 2011; Frias-Martinez et al., 2012; Steenbruggen et al., 2015).

These limitations reflect some wider issues that have been raised about the use of Big Data in the social sciences (boyd and Crawford, 2012; Lyon, 2014; Kitchin, 2014; Leszczynski and Crampton, 2016; Symons and Alvarado, 2016). The "black-box" nature of Big Data and the considerable hardware and software resources necessary for their analysis are among the main causes for concern: not only does this place increasing demands on researchers to obtain the knowledge and skills necessary to operate the hardware and software (which can, arguably, be addressed by increasing budgets and collaboration), it may also lead to outsourcing of the more technical parts of research, leading to loss of control and understanding—by researchers—of data compilation, extraction, and analysis (Miller, 2010; Tranos and Nijkamp, 2013; Dourish, 2016).

Many researchers feel that this lack of technical understanding—due not only to the data's size and complexity, but also to their proprietary nature—will limit their capacity to analyze and interpret them. Notwithstanding these epistemological questions, other researchers suggest that these problems are essentially technical, which, once resolved, will allow Big Data to be used to improve cities by enabling real-time exploration, providing information and helping identify patterns that could be used to predict future problems (Batty, 2013; Townsend, 2013; Eagle and Greene, 2014).

This difference of approach reflects two different uses of Big Data. Doubts emanate from researchers seeking to understand social and economic processes, whereas those interested in observing and managing infrastructure, networks, and flows, express optimism. Where these two different uses of Big Data intersect—and we suggest that the study of workplace mobility is one of them—there is some confusion: the possibilities of Big Data that are touted by some are considered over-optimistic by others.

For example, there is widespread belief that Big Data can support better decision-making by helping to identify stakeholders, to find likely partners, and to form relationships, thereby enabling cities and city planners to better address the needs of multiple actors (Townsend, 2013; Goldsmith and Crawford, 2014). Policymakers are increasingly drawn to the Smart City framework without much evidence of its actual benefits (Kitchin, 2013; Greenfield, 2013). As appealing as Big Data and their analytical tools and methods are, there is uncertainty as to what kinds of conclusions can actually be drawn from them. It has been argued that, mesmerized by Big Data, contextual, political, emotional, and other motivations are being overlooked by the optimists (boyd and Crawford, 2012; Marshall, 2015; Shearmur, 2015). Cities making policy decisions based on data and correlations are at risk of misinterpreting causality, for people and their interactions cannot be reduced to the equivalent of billiard balls (Graham and Shelton, 2013; Greenfield, 2013).

These researchers question the extent to which Big Data can really further our understanding of urban processes—which is not the same thing as their observation. MIT SENSEable City Lab, the Center for Complex Network Research/BarabásiLab and the University of Tartu, for instance, have pioneered research on the urban metabolism with the use of Call Data Records (CDR). These are metadata: they consist of the origin and destination of calls, as well as their timestamp, the duration of the call, and the status of the caller (worker, non-worker, or student). CDR promises information on population clusters, travel patterns, and temporal clusters of activities, which, when combined with demographic data and land-use plans, can produce an image of the city and how it is being used by certain groups of individuals (Ratti et al., 2006; Calabrese et al., 2010; Becker et al., 2011, Ahas et al., 2015). Yet these data remain passive, lack texture, and are opportunistic. The quality of CDR depends largely on the presence of cell towers within the desired area of study. Data are generated only when an exchange or transaction occurs, the underlying assumption being that these digital transactions are sufficient for obtaining an understanding of how the city works; without denying that interesting information is indeed obtained about phone calls, it is unclear exactly what else is being observed and what the underlying processes and motivations of the individuals and groups are (Steenbruggen et al., 2015). Furthermore, the data are not open source, and privacy regulations grant limited access to researchers; and, of course, it is difficult to determine the type of activity or exchange (personal or professional, and in what sector) taking place through CDR alone.

A recent paper by van Meeteren and Poorthuis (2017) uses Twitter data to test the Christallerian behavior of urban consumers. While these data are more easily available than CDR, and while the study's results are promising, they conclude that:

> We could only reach our conclusions after considerable effort and end up with a very partial geography, with limited relevance to the local population and policy makers. This alerts us to the fact that although Big Data is a defining phenomenon of our times, it requires critical scrutiny … and we should be wary of embracing it as a panacea that can replace "traditional" data gathering and analysis. (van Meeteren and Poorthuis (2017: 22)

Considerable effort is being invested in developing new data mining techniques, and in exploring other sources of data (see Yao et al., 2016), such as noise and mobility sensors, but it remains unclear what impact this will have on social scientific understandings of the city.

Can Big Data Track Where Work Actually Takes Place?

Given these characteristics of Big Data, to what extent can they be used to investigate the intra-urban daytime mobility of workers? In their current state, are they adapted to investigating such a question?

So far Big Data have proven useful at establishing correlations between fairly simple things—for instance, while it requires huge amounts of data to predict which types of New York manhole cover will blow up (Mayer-Schönberger and Cukier, 2013) the independent variable—a manhole cover blowing—is straightforward. Likewise, understanding traffic flows is highly complex, but can be based on large numbers of simultaneous, but straightforward, traffic counts (see Reades et al., 2016; Zhong et al., 2016). Social phenomena can usually not be reduced to such straightforward events and counts. Even if Big Data are used to merely observe (e.g., see the methodology developed by Ahas et al., 2015), rather than explain, workplace mobility, this requires grasping the content of communications and understanding what people are actually doing at a given time and in a given place: someone can be sitting at a café working on a computer (reading an article on job location, for example), and his/her neighbor can be sitting near-by doing exactly the same thing, but for leisure purposes. We briefly outline three limitations of Big Data with respect to the study of where work takes place across the city.

1. What are different workers' levels of mobility and motility (mobility potential)? Big Data provide metadata, not specific information about the user such as employment status (full time versus part time), the profession (entrepreneur versus technician), or the industry (higher tier services versus lower tier services, knowledge-intensive or labor-intensive). This makes it difficult to understand the level of mobility of different types of workers using Big Data alone. These data provide new—inductive and correlation-based—insights into how particular networks function, together with limited information on the users of these networks. But these data provide no information about the possibilities open to each worker: for instance, doing work at Starbucks out of choice is fundamentally different from working there because one has not been provided with an office.

2. What kind of work-related activities do mobile workers perform? Not all economic activity is mediated by technology: interacting with people directly, meeting them face-to-face, negotiating, collaborating, and discussing are key work activities that are not digitally recorded. Likewise, reading a (paper) report or book can be an economic activity that occurs off-line but is nonetheless mobile (Lyons and Urry, 2005). It is thus one thing to know where people are at each moment of the day (something that mobile phone operators could conceivably record for people with a mobile phone turned on and who are within range), but quite another to know *why* they are where they are and *what* they are doing there. By focusing on user information extracted from ICTs, we risk overlooking a level of mobility of work that does not rely on technology for workplace mobility.

3. Can Big Data illuminate individual mobile worker trajectories? Even if tracking data were used to address the more straightforward question of tracking the movement through the day of employed people, this cannot be done without identifying which phone users are employed, and which are working on a given day. Furthermore, one would need to make assumptions about how representative the workers being tracked (i.e., those with a phone turned on) are of all workers. In other words, it is not raw phone data (even if the actual content of conversations is known), but data crossed with information about the individuals in whose pocket the phone is sitting and their current activities that could begin to reveal information about where work activity takes place within the city. Strictly speaking, raw data can track where phones that are switched on are located throughout the day; maybe—assuming no confidentiality issues—what is said during conversations, and the location of the person being called can also be accessed. By assuming the phone is in the pocket of the owner, and by crossing phone data with information gleaned from social networks, somewhat more complex inferences can be made. This type of analysis could provide new ideas about ways cities function, but cannot address the question that is central to this paper, and cannot verify that the ideas outlined in the first section are correct. It is also plagued with confidentiality issues that are virtually insurmountable since it would require the *content* of communications being analyzed.

While there is little doubt that Big Data can be a useful tool in furthering our understanding of worker mobility, they have yet to be properly harnessed and put to use as a tool for understanding social and economic questions relevant to city analysts and managers. The paradox—at least for those who put great stock in Big Data—is that these data can only be used to study processes that are already well understood (such as Christaller's theory of consumer behavior). They are less well suited to explore novel phenomena that are in the process of being conceptualized. For the time being, the way economic value is generated along trajectories by urban workers has not been studied and is not well understood. This requires qualitative work on the ways in which work location and work-life balance are changing; such research will provide some insight into the changing location of economic activity. It is only once the phenomenon is well understood that relevant indicators can be devised, and information drawn from Big Data used—as one tool among others—to track certain aspects of the phenomenon.

Conclusion

Technology is undoubtedly changing the face of the city. The creation of cyberspace, or cyberplace (Batty, 1997), has led to the detachment of some economic activity from physical space. This detachment is, however, partial. It is not that we no longer use space to perform work, but that the typology of space, or rather spaces, of work varies. Today, people can work at an office, from their homes, at a café, from a subway, or train station—their work taking place along a trajectory during the day. It has become more difficult to pinpoint where work, most especially knowledge work, takes place. As the idea of a fixed place of work begins to fade, urban planners need to concern themselves with the fate of workplaces that are no longer desirable, nor affordable, for firms as well as individuals. To do so, knowledge on employment location needs to be renewed.

Data and research methods traditionally used for the study of employment location are no longer suited to the task. In this paper we discuss whether Big Data derived from ICTs—that also enable workplace mobility—can be used to trace geographical trajectories of mobile workers.

We argue that the questions pertaining to workplace mobility, and of where value-creation actually takes place in the city cannot be resolved by passively observing movement: this can provide some ideas, some hypotheses, but it is only by performing more qualitative, on-site observational and ethnographic studies that one can begin to understand how individuals separate work from other activities, and where these different types of activity take place in space and along trajectories.

One of the current dangers of Big Data is that they are being used to define questions being asked, rather than as tools to generate knowledge about socially relevant questions. The enthusiasm generated in some quarters by these new data, enthusiasm fueled not only by the possibilities they offer to better understand some urban phenomena but also by the economic interests they further, have tended to overwhelm basic methodological and epistemological precepts.

Furthermore, the distinction between correlations and causes is an important one: at the very least, causal analysis requires theory and an understanding of social mechanisms and interactions. Correlations can support and confirm theories, but can rarely produce them. Inductive methods, which are a long-standing and valid approach to theory building, do not obviate the need to build the theories themselves, nor the need to verify and test them by means that extend beyond just more correlations (Calude and Longo, 2016). While the end of theory has been touted by some prominent technophiles (Anderson, 2008) and furthers the interests and ambitions of corporations that profit from this type of belief (Simonite, 2014), there is skepticism in the researcher community about these claims: Big Data, their size and newness notwithstanding, have not altered basic epistemological precepts. They have however, ushered in renewed respectability for inductive reasoning. They present many opportunities, as well as challenges, for research, and more attention should be paid to ways in which Big Data can be paired to theory, and matched to other data and to qualitative work, to produce more concrete images of changing urban dynamics.

Workplace mobility—the process which we, as researchers interested in the urban economy, would like to better document and understand—is a reflection of wider social and economic trends: the economic function of places in the city carries implications for planning practice. Given our belief—confirmed by a close reading of the literature, by theoretical reasoning, but not yet by empirical work—that the methods we have previously used to study the geography of urban economic activity are not able to capture the key phenomenon of workplace mobility, our initial idea was to turn towards Big Data such as Twitter feeds or cellphone metadata.

The more we considered this, the more it became evident that we currently have insufficient knowledge about workplace mobility to devise sensible indicators or to interpret the data. In this paper we have outlined the reasons why Big Data are not yet appropriate for this type of research. In doing so, we have touched upon wider questions that pertain to the nature of these data and to the nature of the knowledge that they generate. This contributes to debates about what these data can reveal, what they cannot, how they can be accessed, and whether they can be analyzed without recourse to "black-box" algorithms.

Of course, ever since Anderson's (2008) provocative assertion that Big Data are ushering in the end of theory, and as Big Data have become widespread and (partially) available, these questions have been discussed by many other researchers. The key contribution of this paper is to move beyond fundamental, but abstract, epistemological discussions of the possibilities and pitfalls of Big Data, in order to assess, for a specific question—the apparently straightforward one of where work actually takes place—what Big Data can and cannot contribute.

Bibliography

R. Ahas, A. Aasa, Y. Yuan, M. Raubal, Z. Smoreda, Y. Liu, C. Ziemlicki, M. Tiru, M. Zook, "Everyday Space–Time Geographies: Using Mobile Phone-Based Sensor Data to Monitor Urban Activity in Harbin, Paris, and Tallinn," *International Journal of Geographical Information Science* 29: 11 (2015) 2017–2039.

A. Agrawal, I. Cockburn, and J. McHale, "Gone But Not Forgotten: Knowledge Flows, Labor Mobility, and Enduring Social Relationships," *Journal of Economic Geography* 6: 5 (2006) 571–591.

C. Anderson, "The End of Theory: The Data Deluge Makes the Scientific Method Obsolete," *Wired* (June 23, 2008) http://www.uvm.edu/~cmplxsys/wordpress/wp-content/uploads/reading-group/pdfs/2008/anderson2008.pdf Accessed March 15, 2017.

M. Augé, *Non-Place: Introduction to an Anthropology of Supermodernity* [1992], translated by John Howe (London: Verso, 1995).
H. Bathelt and P. Turi, "Local, Global and Virtual Buzz: The Importance of Face-to-face Contact in Economic Interaction and Possibilities To Go Beyond," *Geoforum* 42: 5 (2011) 520–529.
M. Batty, "Virtual Geography," *Futures* 29: 4 (1997) 337–352.
M. Batty, "Urban Modeling," in *International Encyclopedia of Human Geography* (Oxford, UK: Elsevier, 2009) 51–58.
M. Batty, *The New Science of Cities* (Cambridge, MA, USA: MIT Press, 2013).
J. O. Baerenholdt, "Governmobility: the Powers of Mobility," *Mobilities* 8: 1 (2013) 20–34.
R. A. Becker et al., "A Tale of One City: Using Cellular Network Data For Urban Planning," *IEEE Pervasive Computing* 10: 4 (2011) 18–26.
J. Bennett, et al., "Workplace Impact of Social Networking," *Property Management* 28: 3 (2010) 138–148.
L. Boltanski and E. Chiapello, *the New Spirit of Capitalism* (London: Verso, 2005).
E. Borg and J. Söderlund. "Moving in, Moving On: Liminality Practices in Project-Based Work," *Employee Relations* 36: 2 (2013) 182–197.
D. Boyd and K. Crawford, "Critical Questions for Big Data: Provocations for a Cultural, Technological, and Scholarly Phenomenon," *Information, Communication & Society* 15: 5 (2012) 662–679.
B. Brown and K. O'Hara, "Place as a Practical Concern of Mobile Workers," *Environment and Planning A* 35: 9 (2003) 1565–1587.
M. Castells, *The Rise of the Network Society: the Information Age: Economy, Society, and Culture*, Vol. 1. (Oxford: John Wiley & Sons, 2011).
F. Calabrese et al., "Urban Computing and Mobile Devices," *IEEE Pervasive Computing* 6: 3 (2007) 52–57.
F. Calabrese, F.C. Pereira, G. Di Lorenzo, L. Liu, C. Ratti, "The Geography of Taste: Analyzing Cell Phone Mobility and Social Events," in eds. P. Floréen, A. Krüger, M. Spasojević, "Pervasive Computing: Lecture Notes in Computer Science" (Berlin, Heidelberg: Springer, 2010) 22–37.
C. Calude and G. Longo, "The Deluge of Spurious Correlation in Big Data," Foundations of Science (2016) online, doi:10.1007/s10699-016-9489-4
P. Capelli and J. R. Keller, "Classifying Work in the New Economy," *Academy of Management Review* 38: 4 (2013) 575–596.
N. Cook, "The Insecure World of Freelancing," *the Atlantic* (July 25, 2015).
G. Cooper et al., "Mobile Society? Technology, Distance and Presence," in S. Woolgar, ed., *Virtual Society? Technology, Cyberbole, Reality* (Oxford: Oxford University Press, 2002) 286–301.
E. Currid, *The Warhol Economy: How Fashion, Art, and Music Drive New York City* (Princeton: Princeton University Press, 2007).
J. Deal, D. G. Altman, and S. G. Rogelberg, "Millennials at Work: What We Know and What We Need To Do (If Anything)," *Journal of Business and Psychology* 25: 2 (2010) 191–199.
P. Delort, *Le Big Data* (Paris: Presses Universitaires de France, 2015).
E. Demerouti et al., "New Ways of Working: Impact on Working Conditions, Work–Family Balance, and Well-Being," in *The Impact of ICT on Quality of Working Life* (Netherlands: Springer, 2014) 123–141.
P. Dourish, "the Internet of Urban Things," in eds. R. Kitchin and S-Y. Perng, *Code and the City* (New York: Routledge, 2016) 27–48.
N. Eagle and K. Greene, *Reality Mining: Using Big Data to Engineer a Better World* (Cambridge, MA, USA: MIT Press, 2014).
D. Feinlieb, *Big Data Boot Camp* (New York: Apress, 2014).
A. Felstead, "Rapid Change or Slow Evolution? Changing Places of Work and Their Consequences in the UK," *Journal of Transport Geography* 21 (2012) 31–38.
A. Felstead et al., "The Shifting Locations of Work: New Statistical Evidence on the Spaces and Places of Employment," *Work, Employment and Society* 19: 2 (2005) 415–431.
E. Finn, *What Algorithms Want* (Cambridge, MA: MIT Press, 2017).

R. Florida, *the Great Reset: How New Ways of Living and Working Drive Post-Crash Prosperity* (Canada: Random House, 2010).

G. Friedman, "Workers Without Employers: Shadow Corporations and the Rise of the Gig Economy," *Review of Keynesian Economics* 2 (2014) 171–188.

V. Frias-Martinez et al., "Estimation of Urban Commuting Patterns using Cellphone Network Data," *Proceedings of the ACM SIGKDD International Workshop on Urban Computing*, (Beijing ACM, 2012) 9–16.

J. Glücker, "Islands of Expertise: Global Knowledge Transfer in a Technology Service Firm," in H. Bathelt, M. Feldmann, and D. Kogler, eds, *Beyond Territory* (London: Routledge, 2011) 207–226.

S. Goldsmith and S. Crawford, *the Responsive City: Engaging Communities through Data-Smart Governance* (San Francisco, CA, USA: Hoboken, NJ: Jossey-Bass, 2014).

I. Gordon and P. McCann, "Industrial Clusters: Complexes, Agglomeration and/or Social Networks," *Urban Studies* 37: 3 (2000) 513–532.

M. Graham and T. Shelton, "Geography and the Future of Big Data, Big Data and the Future of Geography," *Dialogues in Human Geography* 3: 3 (2013) 255–261.

A. Greenfield, *Against the Smart City* (New York: Do Projects, 2013).

S. Halford, "Hybrid Workspace: Re-Spatialisations of Work, Organization and Management," *New Technology* 20: 1 (2005) 19–33.

J. V. Hall and A. B. Krueger, "An Analysis of the Labor Market for Uber's Driver-Partners in the United States" (Princeton University Industrial Relations Section Working Paper 587, 2015).

T. Hägerstrand, "Diorama, Path and Project", *Tidschriftvoor Economieen Sociale Geografie* (1982) 73:6

S. L. Handy and P. L. Mokhtarian, "Planning for Telecommuting Measurement and Policy Issues," *Journal of the American Planning Association* 61: 1 (1995) 99–111.

D. Helbing, "What the Digital Revolution Means for Us," in *Thinking Ahead: Essays on Big Data, Digital Revolution, and Participatory Market Society* (Switzerland: Springer International, 2015) 177–187.

D. Hislop and C. Axtell, "The Neglect of Spatial Mobility in Contemporary Studies of Work: the Case of Telework," *New Technology, Work and Employment* 22: 1 (2007) 34–51.

D. Hislop and C. Axtell, "To Infinity and Beyond? Workspace and the Multi-Location Worker," *New Technology, Work and Employment* 24: 1 (2009) 60–75.

D. Hislop, "Driving, Communicating and Working: Understanding the Work-Related Communication Behaviours of Business Travellers on Work-Related Car Journeys," *Mobilities* 8: 2 (2013) 220–237.

F. Huber, "Do Clusters Really Matter For Innovation Practices in Information Technology? Questioning the Significance of Technological Knowledge Spillovers," *Journal of Economic Geography* 12: 1 (2012) 107–126.

J. Hwang and R. J. Sampson, "Divergent Pathways of Gentrification Racial Inequality and the Social Order of Renewal in Chicago Neighborhoods," *American Sociological Review* 79: 4 (2014) 726–751.

J. E. Katz and M. Aakhuis, *Perpetual Contact: Mobile Communication, Private Talk, Public Performance* (Cambridge, UK: Cambridge University Press, 2002).

S. Kesselring, "Pioneering Mobilities: New Patterns of Movement and Motility in a Mobile World," *Environment and Planning A* 38: 2 (2006) 269–279.

S. Kesselring, "Corporate Mobilities Regimes: Mobility, Power and the Socio-Geographical Structurations of Mobile Work," *Mobilities* 10: 4 (2015) 571–591.

R. Kitchin, "Big Data and Human Geography: Opportunities, Challenges and Risks," *Dialogues in Human Geography* 3: 3 (2013): 262–267.

R. Kitchin, "Big Data, New Epistemologies and Paradigm Shifts," *Big Data & Society* 1: 1 (2014) 1–12.

R. Kitchin and G. McArdle, "What Makes Big Data, Big Data? Exploring the Ontological Characteristics of 26 Datasets," *Big Data and Society* 3: 1 (2016) 1–10.

H. Krahn and G. S. Lowe, *Literacy Utilization in Canadian Workplaces* (Canada: Statistics Canada, 1998).

M.-P. Kwan, "Time, Information Technologies, and the Geographies of Everyday Life," *Urban Geography* 23: 5 (2002) 471–482.

C. Lassen, "Networking, Knowledge Organizations and Aeromobility," *Geografiska Annaler: Series B, Human Geography* 91: 3 (2009) 229–243.

A. Leszczynski and J. Crampton, "Introduction: Spatial Big Data and Everyday Life," *Big Data & Society* 3: 2 (2016) 1–6.

C. Licoppe, "Connected Presence: The Emergence of a New Repertoire For Managing Social Relationships in a Changing Communication Technoscape," *Environment and Planning D: Society and Space* 22: 1 (2004) 135–156.

B. Loacker and M. Śliwa, "Moving to Stay in the Same Place?' Academics and Theatrical Artists as Exemplars of the 'Mobile Middle," *Organization* 23: 5 (2015) 657–679.

D. Lyon, "Surveillance, Snowden, and Big Data: Capacities, Consequences, Critique," *Big Data & Society* 1: 2 (2014) 1–13.

G. Lyons and J. Urry, "The Use and Value of Travel Time," Unpublished manuscript (2004).

G. Lyons and J. Urry, "Travel Time Use in the Information Age," *Transportation Research Part A: Policy and Practice* 39: 2 (2005) 257–276.

G. Lyons et al., "Comparing Rail Passengers' Travel Time Use in Great Britain between 2004 and 2010," *Mobilities* 8: 4 (2013) 560–579.

M. Mahrt and M. Scharkow, "the Value of Big Data in Digital Media Research," *Journal of Broadcasting & Electronic Media* 57: 1 (2013) 20–33.

A. Marshall, "Why Most Twitter Maps Can't Be Trusted," *CityLab* (March 26, 2015).

R. Martin and P. Sunley, "Deconstructing Clusters: Chaotic Concept Or Policy Panacea?" *Journal of Economic Geography* 3: 1 (2003) 5–35.

D. Massey et al., "Academic–Industry Links and Innovation: Questioning the Science Park Model," *Technovation* 12: 3 (1992) 161–175.

D. Massey, *For Space* (CA: Sage, 2005).

V. Mayer-Schönberger and K. Cukier, *Big Data: A Revolution That Will Transform How We Live, Work, and Think* (New York, USA: Houghton Mifflin Harcourt, 2013).

M. van Meeteren and A. Poorthuis. "Christaller and 'Big Data': Recalibrating Central Place Theory Via the Geoweb," *Urban Geography* online (2017) doi:10.1080/02723638.2017.1298017

E. J. Meijers, "From Central Place to Network Model: Theory and Evidence of a Paradigm Change," *Tijdschrift voor economische en sociale geografie* 98: 2 (2007) 245–259.

H. J. Miller, "The Data Avalanche Is Here: Shouldn't We Be Digging?". *Journal of Regional Science* 50: 1 (2010) 181–201.

C. Miller and C. Rampell. "Yahoo Orders Home Workers Back To the Office," *The New York Times* (February 25, 2013).

J. Nilles, *Making Telecommuting Happen: A Guide For Telemanagers and Telecommuters* (New York: Van Nostrand Reinhold, 1994).

D. Nunan and M.-L. Di Domenico, "Market Research and the Ethics of Big Data," *International Journal of Market Research* 55: 4 (2013) 2–13.

J. B. Parr, "Agglomeration Economies: Ambiguities and Confusions," *Environment and Planning A* 34: 4 (2002) 717–731.

H. Rainie and B. Wellman, *Networked: The New Social Operating System* (Cambridge: MIT Press, 2012).

M. Rathore et al., "Urban Planning and Building Smarter Cities Based On the Internet of Things Using Big Data Analytics," *Computer Networks* 101 (2016) 63–80.

C. Ratti, et al., "Mobile Landscapes: Using Location Data From Cell Phones For Urban Analysis," *Environment and Planning B: Planning and Design* 33: 5 (2006) 727–748.

J. Reades, F. Calabrese, and C. Ratti, "Eigenplaces: Analyzing Cities Using the Space–Time Structure of the Mobile Phone Network," *Environment and Planning B* 36: 5 (2009) 824–836.

J. Reades et al., "Finding Pearls in London's Oysters," *Built Environment* 42: 3 (2016) 365–381.

R. B. Reich, *The Work of Nations: Preparing Ourselves for 21st Century Capitalism* (New York: Vintage Books, 1992).

S. Schieman and M. Young, "The Demands of Creative Work: Implications for Stress in the Work–Family Interface," *Social Science Research* 39: 2 (2010) 246–259.

R. Sennett, "Growth and Failure: the New Political Economy and its Culture," in eds. M. Featherstone and S. Lash, *Spaces of Culture: City, Nation, World* ... 14–26 (London: Sage, 1999).

R. Shearmur, "Innovation, Regions and Proximity: From Neo-Regionalism To Spatial Analysis," *Regional Studies* 45: 9 (2011) 1225–1243.

R. Shearmur, "the Geography of Intrametropolitan KIBS Innovation: Distinguishing Agglomeration Economies from Innovation Dynamics," *Urban Studies* 49: 11 (2012) 2331–2356.

R. Shearmur, "Dazzled by Data: Big Data, the Census and Urban Geography," *Urban Geography* 36: 7 (2015) 965–968.

R. Shearmur et al., "Intrametropolitan Employment Structure: Polycentricity, Scatteration, Dispersal and Chaos in Toronto, Montreal and Vancouver, 1996–2001," *Urban Studies* 44: 9 (2007) 1713–1738.

M. Sheller and J. Urry, "The New Mobilities Paradigm," *Environment and Planning A* 38: 2 (2006) 207–226.

T. Shelton, A. Poorthuis, and M. Zook, "Social Media and the City: Rethinking Urban Socio-Spatial Inequality Using User-Generated Geographic Information," *Landscape and Urban Planning* 142 (2015) 198–211.

T. Simonite, "Google's Intelligence Designer," *MIT Technology Review* (December 2, 2014) http://www.technologyreview.com/news/532876/googles-intelligence-designer/ Accessed November 3, 2016.

J. Steenbruggen, E. Tranos, and P. Nijkamp, "Data from Mobile Phone Operators: A Tool for Smarter Cities?" *Telecommunications Policy* 39: 3 (2015) 335–346.

L. Suarez-Villa and W. Walrod, "Operational Strategy, R&D and Intra-Metropolitan Clustering in a Polycentric Structure: The Advanced Electronics Industries of the Los Angeles Basin," *Urban Studies* 34: 9 (1997) 1343–1380.

J. Symons and R. Alvarado, "Can We Trust Big Data? Applying Philosophy of Science to Software," *Big Data & Society* 3: 2 (2016) doi:2053951716664747.

S. Taylor and A. Spicer, "Time for Space: A Narrative Review of Research on Organizational Spaces," *International Journal of Management Reviews* 9: 4 (2007) 325–346.

A. Torre, "On the Role Played By Temporary Geographical Proximity in Knowledge Transmission," *Regional Studies* 42: 6 (2008) 869–889.

A. M. Townsend, *Smart Cities: Big Data, Civic Hackers, and the Quest for a New Utopia* (New York: WW Norton & Co, 2013).

E. Tranos and P. Nijkamp, "the Death of Distance Revisited: Cyberplace, Physical and Relational Proximities," *Journal of Regional Science* 53: 5 (2013) 855–873.

E. Tranos and P. Nijkamp, "Mobile Phone Usage in Complex Urban Systems: A Space-Time, Aggregated Human Activity Study," *Journal of Geographical Systems* 17: 2 (2015) 157–185.

J. Urry, *Mobilities* (UK: Polity, 2007).

B. Waber, J. Magnolfi, and G. Lindsay. "Workspaces that Move People." *Harvard Business Review* 92: 10 (2014) 68–77.

M. R. Warner, "Asking Tough Questions About the Gig Economy," *Washington Post* (June 18, 2015).

Y. Yao, X. Li, X. Liu, P. Liu, Z. Liang, J. Zhang, K. Mai, "Sensing Spatial Distribution of Urban Land Use By Integrating Points-of-Interest and Google Word2Vec Model," *International Journal of Geographical Information Science* 31: 4 (2016) 1–24.

C. Zhong et al., "Variability in Regularity: Mining Temporal Mobility Patterns in London, Singapore and Beijing using Smart-Card Data," *Plos one* 11: 2 (2016) doi:e0149222.

Index

Note: Page numbers in *italics* refer to figures
Page numbers in **bold** refer to tables
Page numbers followed by "n" refer to endnotes

accessibility 10
Adham, K. 88
Anderson, C. 111
Armondi, Simonetta 1, 27
Augé, M. 103

Baidu.com 71
Becky, P.Y. 2
Big Data 100; algorithms 101; "black-box" nature of 107; dangers of 110; limitations 109; tracking 108–10; urban studies 101, 106–8
Bilandzic, M. 11
Boltanski, L. 102
Brown, B. 11
Bruzzese, A. 1, 27, 28

Café Köket 13–15; contracts types *18*; fields of primary occupation *17*; reasons for working in 17–20; spatial characteristics of 15–17; teleworkers 17–20
call data records (CDR) 107–8
Capelli, P. 102
Castells, M. 89, 103
CDR *see* call data records (CDR)
central business district (CBD) of Lujiazui 78
Chiapello, E. 102
China: co-working offices 71–3, *72*, 78–80, *79*; innovation in 69, 70, 81; venture capital holders in 68, 80
China Internet Network Information Center (CNNIC) 67
coffee shops 5–7, 10–11
commuting workers, micro-urban network of 6
contracts 101; temporary 101, 104
co-working environments 6
co-working offices, Shanghai (China): actors in 71–3, *72*; development 73, 81; locational choice of 78–80, *79*; locational factor for 71, 79–80; networks in *72*; potential investment relations and knowledge transfer 73–5; slogans of **77**; users of 71
co-working spaces (CSs) 6, 7, 10–12, 19–20; paid 12, *13*, 21
co-working spaces (CSs), Milan 48–9, 52–3, 58, 63n5; characteristics and attractiveness **56**; density of *55*; development 51; emergence and diffusion of 49–52; as innovative workplaces 63n1; location patterns 52–7; methodology and research questions 52–3; proliferation of 53–4; urban agglomerations of *56*; urban and local effects **59**; urban scale 60
creative production, Milan 28, 31, 35–8
CSs *see* co-working spaces (CSs)
cultural industry, Milan 35
cyberplace 110
cyberspace 110

Deck 12
Della Dora, V. 87
den Heijer, A. 93
Deskmag (2015) 69
digital Bohemians 11
digital economies 47
digital industrial revolution 47
Di Marino, Mina 1
Di Vita, Stefano 1, 2, 47
Dubai: palm projects 87; urban megaprojects 87
"Dubaification" 87
"Dubaization" 87

economic geography, Milan 30–1
Education City in Doha *90*, 90–4, *92*, **93**
emerging workplaces 20
entrepreneurs, non-local 75
Evans, J. 93
Evolutionary Economic Geography framework 50
Ewers, M.C. 87

INDEX

fab lab (fabrication laboratory) 40n1, 50
The FabLab 61
F2F communication 76, 77
Finland 12–13
Foth, M. 11
FrabiQ incubator 34–5
Friebe, H. 11
Friedman, G. 102
Fuorisalone 37, 41n15

Gellert, P.K. 88, 91
Graham, S. 94
group member interactions 75–7
Gulf region: economies, Knowledge Megaprojects transform 94–5; from "Instant Urbanism" to knowledge megaprojects in 87–90, *89*; Knowledge Megaprojects 90

Habermas, J. 8
Hall, P. 89
Hampton, K.N. 8
Hanley, Richard 2
Hartmann, M. 11
Helsinki 12, *14*; geographical distribution of *14*; public libraries in 14; urban functions in *16*; urban offices in *13*; Vision 2050 12
Helsinki Think Company 12, 14–15; contracts types *18*; fields of primary occupation *17*; reasons for working in 17–20; spatial characteristics of 15–17; teleworkers of 18
Hollands, R.G. 29
HUB13 12
hybrid workplaces 10–11

information and communication technologies (ICT) 7, 21, 100; development 47–9; importance of 63n11; urban spaces and 9–10
innovation, in China 69, 70, 81
Innovation Works (IW) 71, **77**
innovative workplaces, co-working spaces as 63n1
"Instant Urbanism", to knowledge megaprojects 87–90, *89*
interaction, groups 77–8
International Branch Campuses (IBCs) 88, 89, *89*, 90
Internet 67; Internet entrepreneurs 70; Internet industries 70; "Internet plus" strategy 67–8; users in China 80
Internet start-ups 81
intertwined forces 28
iStart (IS) 71, **77**
Italy 31, 35; economic miracle 30

Jackson, M. 87
Johnson, B. 68

Kallio Library 12
Keller, J.R. 102
KMs *see* Knowledge Megaprojects (KMs)

Knowledge and Technology-Intensive Industries (KTIs), Qatar 86, 90
knowledge-based urban development (KBUD) 87, 89
Knowledge Megaprojects (KMs) 87, 92; instant urbanism to 87–90, *89*; transform Gulf's economies 94–5
Knowledge Precincts (KPs) 91, 92, **93**
Koch, N. 87
König, A. 93
Kontoret 12
Kopomaa, Townsend 9
KPs *see* Knowledge Precincts (KPs)
KTIs *see* Knowledge and Technology-Intensive Industries (KTIs)
Kwan, M.-P. 103

Lapintie, Kimmo 1
libraries 5–7, 10–11; in Helsinki 14
Li Keqiang 67
Loacker, B. 104
Lobo, S. 11
locational factor, for co-working offices 71, 79–80
location patterns, co-working spaces (CSs) 52–7
Lofland, L. 8
Loo, Becky P. Y. 67
Lujiazui, central business district (CBD) 78
Lundvall, B.-Ä. 68
Lynch, B.D. 88, 91

Magasinet Creative Hub 12
Mainio Social and Software Factory 12
Malecki, E.J. 87
Mariotti, Ilaria 2, 47
Marvin, S. 94
Meetingpoint 13–15; contracts types *18*; fields of primary occupation *17*; reasons for working in 17–20; spatial characteristics of 15–17; teleworkers of 18; urban office of 17
Messina, Moriset 11
Metropolitan Area of Helsinki: geographical distribution of *14*; urban offices in *13*
micro-urban network, of commuting workers 6
micro-urban transformation 60
Milan 27; abandonment of areas and buildings in 32; clustering process 35–8; co-working spaces 48–58; creative clusters 49; creative production 28, 31, 35–8; cultural industries in 35; entrepreneurial system 31; local effects **59**; Milan City Council 63n12; Milan IN-policy 34; Milan Smart City 34; Milan Urban Plan (2012) 63n9; Municipal Administration (2016–2021) 62; municipality of 32–4; new policy approach 34; public policy approach 33; self-governing city 53; smart city policy 29, 38, 41n18; smart urban policy between social and spatial 33–5; socio-spatial dynamics and economic geography 30–1; spatial opportunities 31–2; urban change in 28, 33–5, 38–9; urban effects

INDEX

57–60, **59**; urban fabric 32, 63n13; urban regeneration process 29; Zona Tortona 36; *see also* co-working spaces (CSs), Milan
Milieu, with cooperation and competition 77–8
Millennials 10
mobile technologies, impacts of 9
mobile worker trajectories 109
mobility potential 109
Moriset, B. 69
Moser, S. 87
MUDEC 37

Neuberg, Brad 48
new production: dynamics 27; nexus of 33–5
non-local entrepreneurs 75
non-traditional workplaces, proliferation of 22

O'Hara, K. 11
oil drilling technologies 85
Ouis, P. 87

Pacchi, Carolina 2, 47
paid co-working spaces 12, *13*, 21
Pajevic, Filipa 2, 99
People Squared (PS) 71, **77**
Pisapia, Giuliano 33
Polanyi, M. 68
policymakers 107
Ponzini, D. 87
Poorthuis, A. 108
post-functionalist city 6, 7
private spaces 8–9
private spheres 9
public libraries 11; in Helsinki 14
public policy 27; Milan 33
public spaces 8–9; working in 20
public spheres 9
Puro, J.P. 12

Qatar: Knowledge and Technology-Intensive Industries (KTIs) 86, 90; Qatar Foundation 90; "Qatar National Vision 2030" 88
Quarto Oggiaro 35

Rabari, C. 29
Rizzo, A. 2, 87, 88

Sala, Giuseppe 33
self-governing city, Milan 53
semi-central urban areas 29
semi-public spaces 8–9; working in 20
Sennett, R. 102
Shanghai, China 70; co-working offices 71–3, *72*, 78–80, *79*; Internet industries 81; Internet users in 80; *see also* co-working offices, Shanghai (China)
Shearmur, Richard G. 2, 99
Shelton, T. 29
skepticism 110

Sliwa, M. 104
slogans of co-working offices **77**
SLQ *see* State Library of Queensland (SLQ)
smart city notion, re-reading 29
smart city policy, Milan 29, 38, 41n18
sociability level 8
social connectivity 6
social displacement, education city 94
social innovation 34
socio-spatial dynamics 28; Milan 30–1
socio-spatial interpretations 8
State Library of Queensland (SLQ) 11
Storper, M. 29
suburban areas 7
Suhehui (SH) 71, **77**
symbolic analysts 101

Talent Garden Calabiana 61
Tamini, L. 28
Tampere 12
Technopoles of the World (Castells and Hall) 89
teleworkers: Café Köket 17–19; Helsinki Think Company 18; Meetingpoint 18
temporary contracts 101, 104
temporary workplaces 10–11

urban agglomerations, co-working spaces in Milan 56
urban areas, location determinants of service industries in 55
urban change, Milan 27, 28, 33–5, 38–9
urban creativity concept, revisiting 29–30
urban effects, Milan 57–60, **59**
urban fabric, Milan 63n13
urban office 12; of Meetingpoint 17
urban regeneration process, Milan 29
urban scale 59, 60
urban spaces: and information and communication technologies 9–10; social and functional characteristics of 10
urban studies, Big Data and 106–8

value-creation occurs, challenge of locating 101–4
van Meeteren, M. 108
VCHs *see* venture capital holders (VCHs)
Ventura Lambrate 36
venture capital 68; companies 73; firms 78
venture capital holders (VCHs) 69, 73, 75; in China 68, 80

Wang, B. 2, 67
Wi-Fi spots, spatial distribution of public *16*
Work, changes in 101–4
worker mobility 104; dimensions of 104–5; fixed *vs.* unconstrained mobility 105; meetings and face-to-face interactions 104–5; mobility as freedom 105; potential for mobility 105; potential *vs.* actual workplace mobility 105; status and mobility 105; typology 104–6

workers' levels mobility *vs.* motility 109
working: practices 5; in public spaces 20; in semi-public spaces 20
workplace: changes in 101–4; development, alternative 8; mobility 99, 100, 111; technology 99

work-related activities 109
workspaces 27
World Economic Forum, Davos (2014) 67

Yigitcanlar, T. 91, 95